Let's Play Some Bridge

Frank Stewart

MASTER POINT PRESS • TORONTO, CANADA

Master Point Press
214 Merton St. Suite 205
Toronto, Ontario, Canada
M4S 1A6 (647) 956-4933

Email: info@masterpointpress.com
Websites: www.masterpointpress.com
www.teachbridge.com
www.bridgeblogging.com
www.ebooksbridge.com

Library and Archives Canada Cataloguing in Publication

Title: Let's play some bridge / Frank Stewart.
Names: Stewart, Frank, 1946 October 16- author.
Identifiers: Canadiana (print) 20230153968 | Canadiana (ebook) 20230154034 | ISBN 9781771400800
(softcover) | ISBN 9781771405959 (PDF) | ISBN 9781771407397 (EPUB) | ISBN 9781771407892 (Kindle)
Subjects: LCSH: Contract bridge.
Classification: LCC GV1282.3 .S74 2023 | DDC 795.41/5—dc23

Copy editor India Natt Leeming
Interior format Sally Sparrow
Cover design Olena S. Sullivan/New Mediatrix

1 2 3 4 5 6 7 26 25 24 23

Dedication

To my girls, whom nobody could love more.

Acknowledgments

Many of the deals in this book originally appeared in my column in the *Bridge Bulletin*, the American Contract Bridge League (ACBL)'s magazine, and are used with the kind cooperation of that publication. I have had the privilege of being a contributor since 1981 and, for several years, served as an editor. A few deals are adapted from 'Daily Bridge Club', my syndicated column, or from my earlier books. Many have not been published before.

Paul Linxwiler, the current *Bridge Bulletin* Executive Editor, honored me by writing this book's foreword.

Foreword

If there were a Hall of Fame for bridge writers, Frank Stewart would surely be an inductee. For decades, Stewart has authored books, columns in newspapers ('Daily Bridge Club'), and articles in magazines, especially the American Contract Bridge League's *Bridge Bulletin*.

Stewart is widely regarded as an expert analyst, but he possesses a smooth style that allows bridge enthusiasts of all skill levels to follow his instructive explanations of even complex deals.

I have had the privilege of editing Stewart's material in the B*ridge Bulletin* for more than 20 years, and his "over-the-shoulder" descriptions of how good players think when declaring or defending are among the best in the business. Stewart is a master of this style, hugely popular with bridge fans, as it allows a ringside seat into the mind of an expert player as he makes his at-the-table decisions, guided by the clues in the bidding and play.

Whether you're a new player hoping to sharpen your analytical skills or an experienced one who simply enjoys matching wits with a writer, Frank Stewart is a terrific choice.

Paul Linxwiler
Executive Editor, *Bridge Bulletin*

Introduction

When my twenty-fourth book, *Keys to Winning Bridge*, appeared in 2016, I thought it would be my last one. I had nothing more I wanted to say. But I am attracted to the over-the-shoulder approach to presenting a deal. For many years, I have been contributing such a column to the ACBL's *Bridge Bulletin* and I have published two previous over-the-shoulder books. A book of that type is not difficult to put together and Ray Lee was gracious enough to offer to publish it, so I am giving it one more try.

The over-the-shoulder genre became prominent in the writing of Terence Reese and continued in the work of excellent writers such as Mike Lawrence and Larry Cohen. The reader gets access into the mind of an expert and follows his thought processes. The reader is exposed to techniques — such as counting and drawing inferences — that are, supposedly, expert territory.

In my writing, which comprises books, hundreds of magazine articles and, to date, about 11,000 newspaper columns, I focus on logical thinking. Why do we play bridge? Certainly not to memorize a bidding system nor to adhere to an array of rules. The game's appeal lies in problem-solving. During one session, a player faces hundreds of decisions. Some, he can resolve instinctively; but many require reasoning. That is what a player finds exhilarating. He has a problem and figures out the answer.

In this book, most of the deals present problems at a level I would call 'intermediate'. Some of the instructional points appear more than once. For example, following the odds when bidding vulnerable games, making assumptions in the play and using discretion in entering the auction are recurring themes. I won't apologize for that, since repetition is a learning tool.

You will sit with me and be able to compare your decisions with mine. You won't agree with all my actions; bridge involves personal style and judgment. My at-the-table analysis may not even be error-free; that is also part of the game. Still, I hope you will find it instructive to listen in on my thoughts.

Frank Stewart
Fayette, Alabama

Author's note

Tournament partnerships use various systems. One dominant style is Two-over-One, in which a new-suit response at the two-level is forcing to game. Although the bidding in this book is Standard, the focus is on judgment and the commentary is meant to be useful to the reader regardless of the system he favors.

1

In a local Swiss Teams, my partner is a solid citizen in the auction, which may or may not be a good thing since my own style is stodgy as well. Our teammates, however, believe in bidding when it is their turn. Our opponents are veteran club players whose masterpoint totals exceed their skill level. The first two boards look flat; then, with both sides vulnerable, I hold as South:

♠ A K J 6 5 4 3
♡ A
♢ K 9 8
♣ 9 5

East, the dealer, opens 2♡.

My hand is too promising for a 2♠ overcall and too wild to start with a double; I jump to 3♠, suggesting a strong one-suiter. There are no preempts over preempts: any call by me would promise high-card values. If I held:

♠ K Q J 9 6 5 3 ♡ 7 6 ♢ 7 6 5 ♣ 5

I would have to pass.

West passes and my partner cogitates and jumps to 5♠. He thinks we can make a slam if I have a control in hearts and can save us from losing two quick heart tricks. Since I have a first-round control, I am obliged to show it. We might have a grand slam. So I bid 6♡. Partner signs off in 6♠ and I am done. West leads the ♡7.

Dlr: East
Vul: Both

♠ 9 8
♡ J 5 3
◇ A J 7
♣ A K 10 6 2

♠ A K J 6 5 4 3
♡ A
◇ K 9 8
♣ 9 5

West	North	East	South
		2♡	3♠
pass	5♠	pass	6♡
pass	6♠	all pass	

If my partner had held the ♠Q, he might have raised to 7♠. As it was, he didn't like his spade 'support', especially since bad breaks were possible. His 5♠ was aggressive enough since we might well have been off two hearts and (maybe after a trump promotion) a trump trick.

East plays the ♡8 and I take the ace and cash the A-K of trumps. Not unexpectedly, East has a low singleton, so I must avoid a diamond loser to make the slam. Suppose I take the A-K of clubs and ruff a club. All will be well if the suit breaks 3-3 or if a defender happens to hold bare Q-J; otherwise, I expect I will need the diamond finesse.

I lead to the ♣K — both defenders play low — and am about to call for the ♣A, when I stop to reflect. It occurs to me that I may do well to eliminate West's safe exit cards. So instead I ruff a heart and lead a second club: jack, ace, seven. Then I ruff dummy's last heart and exit with a trump to West. The full deal is:

North:
♠ 9 8
♡ J 5 3
◇ A J 7
♣ A K 10 6 2

West:
♠ Q 7 2
♡ 7 6 2
◇ 10 5 4 3 2
♣ J 4

East:
♠ 10
♡ K Q 10 9 8 4
◇ Q 6
♣ Q 8 7 3

South:
♠ A K J 6 5 4 3
♡ A
◇ K 9 8
♣ 9 5

West must lead a diamond — all he has left. Dummy plays low and when East puts up the queen, I am home.

I think the line I chose was best. I would have succeeded if West had held, say, Qxxx in clubs and either the ♦Q or ♦10. If his clubs had been QJxx, I would have hoped for a winning guess in diamonds. (I could judge to play West for 10x since the lead of my last trump would squeeze him in the minors.)

At the other table, my teammate sitting East wasn't satisfied with a mundane 2♥ opening; he tried 3♥. South overcalled 3♠. North liked his hand but he could do no more than raise to 4♠ and there they rested. South took eleven tricks for +650 and we gained 13 IMPs. A mere 26 IMPs were riding on my play in 6♠.

2

In a club duplicate, I have an earnest and competent partner. Only our side is vulnerable and, as South, the dealer, I hold a balanced 19-count.

♠ K Q 4
♡ A Q 4 3
◇ K 8
♣ A J 4 2

I open 1♣, planning to jump to 2NT over a 1◇ or 1♠ response or raise a 1♡ response to 4♡. (Over 1♠, I could reverse into 2♡ but then I would be suggesting longer clubs than hearts, not a balanced hand such as the one I have.)

Our opponents are an active expert pair and West comes in with a 2♣ Michaels cuebid, showing length in the majors, typically 5-5. My partner doubles, telling me the deal belongs to us. East passes.

I suppose I could pass. West will rescue himself to a major, and we might double for a telephone-number penalty. Still, we would have to beat a two-level partial four tricks for +800 to exceed the value of the vulnerable game we can surely make. I hate to let the opponents off the hook and at IMPs, I might pursue a penalty. At matchpoints, I jump to 3NT.

My partner huddles... and raises to 6NT; all pass. West considers his lead and tables the ♠A.

Dlr: South
Vul: N-S

♠ J 7
♡ 9 7
◇ A Q 10 9 6 4
♣ K Q 7

♠ K Q 4
♡ A Q 4 3
◇ K 8
♣ A J 4 2

West	North	East	South
			1♣
2♣	dbl	pass	3NT
pass	6NT	all pass	

West continues with a second spade and I win. East has followed with the five and eight.

This will be an easy make if I bring in the diamonds but, on the auction, a bad split is more than likely. To get some information, I take the ♣AK. West follows, so I can place him with at most one diamond. On the fifth trick, I lead dummy's ♢10 and let it ride. I can do nothing about a 5-0 break and will be doomed if West has the singleton jack — but West follows with the deuce. So, I cross to the ♢K, return to the ♣Q and run the diamonds. Making six. The full deal:

	North	
	♠ J 7 ♡ 9 7 ♢ A Q 10 9 6 4 ♣ K Q 7	
West ♠ A 10 9 3 2 ♡ K 10 8 5 2 ♢ 2 ♣ 9 3	N / W E / S	**East** ♠ 8 6 5 ♡ J 6 ♢ J 7 5 3 ♣ 10 8 6 5
	South ♠ K Q 4 ♡ A Q 4 3 ♢ K 8 ♣ A J 4 2	

The deal furnished ammunition for my opinion that bidding with weak hands often loses. If West doesn't act, we might reach 6NT; but, lacking a crystal ball, I would certainly go down.

Players often enter the auction without considering the possible consequences. When you bid with a flimsy hand — when you are unlikely to buy the contract — you may disrupt the opponents' auction. But you may just as well impel them to bid with all the more determination, reach an unlikely contract and make it because your intervention provided a clue. Edgar Kaplan once analyzed a match and observed thus: "The results... point to a strange conclusion. Could it be that it pays to bid with strong hands and pass with weak ones?"

This is an issue about which I feel strongly; several deals in this book, including the next few, reflect my bias.

3

In a local pairs game, neither side is vulnerable and, as South, I hold:

♠ J 9 8
♡ Q 9 5
◊ 7 4
♣ A J 9 6 4

West, the dealer, passes. My partner opens 1◊, East passes and I respond 1NT. Then, West comes in with 2◊. That is a Michaels cuebid, showing length in both majors with typically five cards in each.

My partner doubles, telling me that the deal belongs to us; we may want to double the opponents for penalty. After two passes, West rescues himself to 2♡ and my partner ponders and bids 3♣. East passes, with what I sense is relief.

I figure I have to act. I have a decent hand and, since the opponents haven't competed vigorously in a major, my partner may have major-suit honors. It's possible we belong in 5♣ or even 6♣ but in a one-session matchpoint game, I can't worry about that. I bid 3NT. If North's hand is wildly distributional, he can overrule me.

Everyone passes and West leads the ♡4.

Dlr: West
Vul: None

♠ A 5
♡ A 7
◊ A K J 6 5
♣ K 5 3 2

♠ J 9 8
♡ Q 9 5
◊ 7 4
♣ A J 9 6 4

West	North	East	South
pass	1◊	pass	1NT
2◊	dbl	pass	pass
2♡	3♣	pass	3NT
all pass			

North put me under pressure with that 3♣ bid. With semi-balanced distribution, great strength and honors everywhere, he could have bid 3NT himself.

I play low from dummy, East contributes the jack and my queen wins. The contract is safe enough but for a good matchpoint result, I may need an overtrick. West presumably has ten major-suit cards — if East had four cards in a major, he would have bid over North's double — so I start with a club to dummy's king. West plays the ten. Next, I take the ♢AK. When both defenders follow low, I can assume West's club was a singleton, so I lead a club to my jack.

West discards, so I finish with 10 tricks — five clubs, two diamonds, two hearts and a spade — for +430. The full deal:

	♠ A 5 ♡ A 7 ♢ A K J 6 5 ♣ K 5 3 2	
♠ K 10 7 4 2 ♡ K 10 8 4 3 ♢ 9 3 ♣ 10	N W E S	♠ Q 6 3 ♡ J 6 2 ♢ Q 10 8 2 ♣ Q 8 7
	♠ J 9 8 ♡ Q 9 5 ♢ 7 4 ♣ A J 9 6 4	

West was unhappy with his partner, maintaining, rather uncharitably, that East should have bid 2♠ over the double as a lead-director. East retorts that it didn't occur to him to bid anything with his junkpile.

West, I think, should have been asking himself why he bid on nothing. The modern 'bid-when-it's-your-turn' competitive style rests on the premise that you have two opponents to confound but only one partner. That style has successes but also losses that its advocates tend to forget — such as when the intervention tells declarer how to play.

At another table in our section, after a similar revealing auction, West did lead a spade against 3NT by South and East took the queen but understandably returned a spade instead of shifting to a heart. Declarer cashed the ♢AK and picked up the clubs. When he ran the clubs, West was in trouble for discards and, at the end, declarer threw him in with a spade to lead from the ♡K, winning ten tricks as I did.

4

In a club duplicate, my partner is moderately experienced and our opponents are intermediates who have ventured into an open game. I wish I saw more 99er players doing that. Facing stronger opposition is a route to improvement and if my opponents produce a good game, they will have a sense of achievement and will be inspired to 'play up' some more. Too many pairs are content to amass masterpoints by playing only in limited games; in my view, they do themselves a disservice.

Neither side is vulnerable and, as South, I pick up:

♠ K J 10 8 7 2
♡ K 5 3 2
♢ —
♣ K J 8

North, the dealer, opens 1NT and my right-hand opponent passes. I can't let this hand go without trying for slam; if my partner has perfect cards, we could be cold for seven. I have all kinds of options. I could respond 2♣ to search for a heart fit but we might belong in spades even if my partner has four hearts. His hand could be:

♠ Q 9 ♡ A 6 5 4 ♢ A 4 2 ♣ A Q 10 6

I could transfer with a 2♡ response and next test the water with a 3♡ bid or a jump to 4♢ as a splinter bid.

With my current partner, I decide on a simpler route. I just jump to 3♠, natural and forcing.

The intermediate to my left comes in with 4♢ and my partner raises to 4♠. Still keen on slam, I continue with a 5♢ cuebid and my partner cogitates and jumps to 6♠. Everyone passes and West leads a trump.

Dlr: North
Vul: None

♠ A 9 5 4
♡ J 6 4
♢ A Q
♣ A Q 10 2

♠ K J 10 8 7 2
♡ K 5 3 2
♢ —
♣ K J 8

West	North	East	South
	1NT	pass	3♠
4♢	4♠	pass	5♢
pass	6♠	all pass	

"I hope you have something in hearts," my partner says. "I've got everything else."

I can't fault his bid, though if my 5♢ bid had been based on a void, his ♢Q had lost value. If only I had a diamond, we would have twelve tricks. As it is, we have only eleven. Leading to the ♡K for a twelfth trick isn't likely to work after West bid at the four-level.

Luckily, I see an option. It's a principle of squeeze play that at least one of the threats must be accompanied by an entry but this may be a rare exception. I start by cashing six rounds of trumps and follow with four clubs. With three tricks left, West has displayed some discomfort and has discarded several diamonds, the ♡10 and ♡Q. So I am sure the position is:

North:
♠ —
♡ J
♢ A Q
♣ —

West:
♠ —
♡ A
♢ K J
♣ —

East:
♠ —
♡ 9 8 7
♢ —
♣ —

South:
♠ —
♡ K 5 3
♢ —
♣ —

I lead the ♡J and West has to win and lead a diamond, giving me the last two tricks. If West had bared the ◇K, I easily could have judged to cash the ◇A on the eleventh trick. The full deal:

	♠ A 9 5 4 ♡ J 6 4 ◇ A Q ♣ A Q 10 2	
♠ 6 ♡ A Q 10 ◇ K J 10 9 7 5 4 ♣ 6 5	N W E S	♠ Q 3 ♡ 9 8 7 ◇ 8 6 3 2 ♣ 9 7 4 3
	♠ K J 10 8 7 2 ♡ K 5 3 2 ◇ – ♣ K J 8	

West asked me whether her 4◇ bid was correct and I answered honestly. Many players would have reflexively tried 4◇ but the bid had little to gain. West wasn't going to buy the contract or take a unilateral sacrifice. The most likely effect of her bid was to guide my play. If West had kept silent, we would still have reached slam but I'm not sure I would have made it. With no clue from the bidding, I might have led up towards the ♡K.

5

In a Regional Stratified Pairs, only our side is vulnerable. I'm playing in a first-time partnership and our system is bare-bones. As South, I hold:

♠ K J
♡ A 6 4
◇ K Q 9 7
♣ A J 6 4

My hopes for a peaceful auction are upset — placid auctions have become rare these days — when West, the dealer, opens 3♠ and two passes follow.

I have no idea what to do. Clearly, we could have a substantial plus available at a game or even a slam. I could double and, if partner passed, I would be satisfied to defend. But if he took out to a four-level contract, I would have to put down my hand in dummy with the lead coming through the ♠KJ. If partner bid 4♡, where my support is deficient and bad breaks are possible, we might go down a bushel.

I think I must act. To avoid being outright stolen from, I must assume that my partner has a share of the missing high-card strength. I try 3NT. I may be down five but at matchpoints, it's only one board and I can just as easily get a zero by passing.

West passes and my partner huddles — and huddles some more. I can understand his hesitation. If you asked a dozen experts what my 3NT bid shows, they might all say, "Who knows?" It's a bid that defies precise definition. I might have risked 3NT with a balanced 16 points. I might have a stronger hand, as here, with which I was reluctant to bid higher. I might have a solid minor suit, a spade stopper and little else. I know players who would risk 3NT with a good hand but no spade stopper, hoping partner would provide one.

Finally, my partner raises to 4NT. I really should pass that. I may have gotten us a decent result when I guessed to bid 3NT. But I would have tried 3NT with a point or two fewer. I could let my partner make the final error by lifting to 5NT… but I go ahead and bid 6NT and all pass. West leads the ♠10 and partner displays the dummy with a shake of his head.

Dlr: West
Vul: N-S

♠ A 5
♡ K 7 3
♢ A 4 3 2
♣ Q 10 9 7

♠ K J
♡ A 6 4
♢ K Q 9 7
♣ A J 6 4

West	**North**	**East**	**South**
3♠	pass	pass	3NT
pass	4NT	pass	6NT
all pass			

It looks as if we need a little luck. I take the ♠A and let the ♣10 ride; West follows low. Next, I lead the ♣9: five, four, eight. Now I have 12 tricks if I can take four in diamonds. Seeking a count of the hand, I lead a heart from dummy and play low. West wins with the nine and leads another spade to my king.

When I cash the ♡AK, West follows, so I can assume his distribution was 7-3-1-2. I lead the ♢A and a second diamond and, when East plays the five and eight, I put in my nine. West shows out and I claim the rest. If East had split his honors on the second diamond, I could have won, cashed the ♣A and gone back to the ♣Q to pick up the diamonds. The full deal:

North:
♠ A 5
♡ K 7 3
♢ A 4 3 2
♣ Q 10 9 7

West:
♠ Q 10 9 8 6 4 3
♡ J 9 2
♢ 6
♣ 8 3

East:
♠ 7 2
♡ Q 10 8 5
♢ J 10 8 5
♣ K 5 2

South:
♠ K J
♡ A 6 4
♢ K Q 9 7
♣ A J 6 4

Most players would have opened 3♠ as West and, indeed, the preempt forced some uncomfortable guesses. Still, it pushed us into an unlikely contract. We had only 31 high-card points and two balanced hands and if we were left alone, I doubt we would have reached slam. Moreover, the preempt helped me win twelve tricks. With no information from the auction, I would have had no reason to discern the diamond position.

6

In the semifinal of a Regional Knockout Teams, we are facing a capable team. Both sides are vulnerable and, as West, I pick up:

♠ K 5
♡ Q 10 8 5
◇ A Q 10 3
♣ 10 8 3

South, the dealer, opens 1♠. I know players who like a swashbuckling approach and would climb in with a double. But though my ♠K looks well placed, sitting over the opening bidder, acting here is too aggressive for my taste. If the opponents have a spade fit, they may outbid us in a competitive auction and then my intervention could help declarer place the cards.

When I pass, North responds 2♣, game-forcing in their style. South rebids 2◇, and North bids 2♠, forcing. South mulls that over, as though he isn't sure what is expected of him, and finally jumps to 4♠. Everyone passes and, displaying great imagination, I lead the ♡5.

Dlr: South
Vul: Both

North:
♠ Q J 3
♡ K 4
◇ 9 6 5
♣ K Q J 5 4

West:
♠ K 5
♡ Q 10 8 5
◇ A Q 10 3
♣ 10 8 3

West	North	East	South
			1♠
pass	2♣	pass	2◇
pass	2♠	pass	4♠
all pass			

Declarer puts up dummy's ♡K, winning, and lets the ♠Q ride to my king.

I can see an easy two-trick set. If South's hand is:

♠ A 10 6 4 2 ♡ A 2 ◇ K J 7 4 ♣ 7 6

I can lead a club; then, when my partner wins and shifts to a diamond, I can take the queen and ace and give him a ruff. Well, getting +200 would be lovely but I must focus on just beating the contract. If declarer has the ♣A, which is quite possible, he has eleven winners and then I must find East with the ◊K. If South has both the ◊K and the ♣A, nothing I can do will stop an overtrick.

A common technique for declarer is to combine his chances. When he has several ways in which he might make the contract, he tries them all in the best order. Combining chances as a defender is uncommon but I can do that here: I shift to the ◊3. Even if declarer has KJxx, we might still beat 4♠. If partner gets in with the ♣A later, he will return a diamond.

As it happens, the full deal is:

	♠ Q J 3 ♡ K 4 ◊ 9 6 5 ♣ K Q J 5 4	
♠ K 5 ♡ Q 10 8 5 ◊ A Q 10 3 ♣ 10 8 3	N W E S	♠ 8 6 2 ♡ J 9 7 6 3 ◊ K 7 ♣ 9 7 6
	♠ A 10 9 7 4 ♡ A 2 ◊ J 8 4 2 ♣ A 2	

We take three diamonds for down one. My defense would have worked even if South had held:

♠A 10 9 7 4 ♡A 2 ◊K J 8 4 2 ♣2

At the other table, my teammates' auction started the same way — they were also playing Two-over-One, despite my entreaties — but over 2♠, South bid 3♣ and North tried 3NT, passed out.

That could have been a winning contract and, in fact, it was. East led the ♡6 and declarer won with the king. When he lost the spade finesse next, West had a problem similar to mine; but with North's solid clubs concealed and the ◊J visible in dummy, a diamond shift was less obvious. Perhaps West should have found the winning defense; but he returned a heart and North wrapped up his game.

7

In a Sectional Knockout Teams, only our side is vulnerable and, as South, I pick up:

♠ A Q
♡ 8 3
◇ A K J 10 4
♣ Q J 6 4

I know notrump hogs who would head for the trough and open 1NT but I see no reason for such a distortion when I expect to be able to describe the hand reasonably well. Moreover, my hand is heavy for a 15-to-17 1NT opening with its good five-card suit and the black-suit honors in combination. So, after East, the dealer, passes, I open 1◇. North responds 1♡ and East comes in with a double.

I have options. I could go ahead and rebid 2♣; but East has promised clubs and 'ignoring the double' in these situations makes no sense to me. Instead, I stake a claim to the deal with a strength-showing redouble.

West takes out to 1♠ and my partner rebids 2♡. He has heart length; I'm not sure how good a hand he has. No doubt he expects me to bid again. I try 2NT. Maybe I should bid 3NT but my redouble did show strength.

North raises to 3NT and all pass. West leads the ♠4.

Dlr: East
Vul: N-S

♠ 5 3
♡ A K J 10 5
◇ 9 8 3
♣ K 5 2

♠ A Q
♡ 8 3
◇ A K J 10 4
♣ Q J 6 4

West	North	East	South
		pass	1◇
pass	1♡	dbl	redbl
1♠	2♡	pass	2NT
pass	3NT	all pass	

East puts up the ♠K and I win.

This looks promising. I can see a line that will make me a favorite for nine tricks. I have six top tricks and can force out the ♣A for two more (but probably not three, since East's double suggested club length). When I win the spade return, I can try a combination shot in the red suits, cashing the ♢AK with the heart finesse in reserve if the ♢Q doesn't fall.

Still, I am mindful of Murphy's Law. (Cy the Cynic, a recurring character in my syndicated column, asserts that when everything has gone wrong with something that could possibly go wrong, it probably wouldn't have worked anyway.) What if both red queens are offside and guarded?

Fortunately, a better play occurs to me. I lead a heart to dummy's ace on the second trick and return the ♣2 through East. If he rises with the ace, I have nine tricks. When he plays low, my queen wins, and then I cash the ♢A, cross to dummy's ♡K and lead the ♢9. East shows out and West's queen scores, but I have four diamonds, two hearts, two spades and a club. The full deal:

	♠ 5 3 ♡ A K J 10 5 ♢ 9 8 3 ♣ K 5 2	
♠ 10 8 6 4 2 ♡ 6 4 ♢ Q 7 6 2 ♣ 7 3	N W E S	♠ K J 9 7 ♡ Q 9 7 2 ♢ 5 ♣ A 10 9 8
	♠ A Q ♡ 8 3 ♢ A K J 10 4 ♣ Q J 6 4	

As I have stated elsewhere in this book, I am struck by how players climb into the auction with no regard for what may happen next. Here, many players would have indulged in East's double but East-West were unlikely to buy the contract or to have a profitable sacrifice. A likely effect of the double was to help North-South judge the bidding or to guide declarer's play, as it did mine. If East keeps silent, we will still reach 3NT; but after a spade lead, I don't know that I would make it. I might lead a club to dummy's king on Trick 2.

At the other table, South chose the off-shape 1NT opening that was anathema to me. North transferred with a 4♦ response, judging that hearts would be an adequate trump suit even if South had two low hearts. West led the ♣7: deuce, eight, jack. Declarer finessed in trumps next and, when East took the queen, continued with the ♣A and a third club. West ruffed but declarer won the spade return, drew trumps and had ten tricks for +620. So, we lost an IMP.

8

In a local Swiss Teams, I have a learning but promising partner. Our opponents are inexperienced but no less earnest. After two uneventful boards, as South, I pick up:

♠ A K J 9 2
♡ A Q 8
◇ A 4 3
♣ 8 4

Both sides are vulnerable. My partner deals and opens 1♣ and right-hand opponent passes.

I can't commit to a slam, especially opposite what people are treating as an opening bid these days; but if partner has a bit of extra strength or shape, we probably have one. What I need to do is elicit his cooperation. So I start with a jump shift to 2♠. In modern bidding, a strong jump shift shows either a self-sustaining suit, a fit for opener's suit or a moderately strong balanced hand. If partner bids 2NT or 3♣ next, I'll bid 3NT and leave any further slam moves to him.

My partner raises to 4♠. I wonder what he has. His normal action with spade support would be a raise to 3♠, leaving more room to investigate. He must have good spade support plus slammish values. It would be defensible for me to jump to 6♠ but, since I'm not totally sure what my partner is doing, I settle for a timid try: I re-raise to 5♠. He should treat that bid as showing both red aces; if I had one or the other, I would cuebid it.

My partner thinks it over and bids 6♠; everyone passes. West leads the ♦J.

Dlr: North
Vul: Both

	North
	♠ Q 10 5 3
	♥ 6
	♦ Q 5 2
	♣ A K J 6 2
	South
	♠ A K J 9 2
	♥ A Q 8
	♦ A 4 3
	♣ 8 4

West	North	East	South
	1♣	pass	2♠
pass	4♠	pass	5♠
pass	6♠	all pass	

Our unscientific bidding has reached a good contract. I think I should have bid 6♠ myself instead of 5♠. Over my 2♠, my partner could have jumped to 4♥, a splinter bid showing spade support and heart shortness. That might have made it easier for us to reach slam.

I suppose that, on the auction, West might have picked an aggressive diamond lead from the king, so I try dummy's queen. Alas, East's king covers and I take the ace. I can see eleven tricks: five trumps in my hand, the red aces, two heart ruffs in dummy and two clubs. But to start, I will try to set up dummy's long clubs. If both black suits break well, I will have no problems; I won't need the heart finesse.

I can afford to take the ♠A; both defenders follow. Next, I cash the ♣AK and ruff a club high. West discards a heart, so I lead a trump to dummy's ten. This time, East discards a heart. I ruff a second club high and lead a trump to the queen, drawing West's last trump. Now, I need the heart finesse; so, after discarding a diamond on the good fifth club, I lead a heart to the queen. Fortunately, it wins and I take the ♥A for my eleventh trick. Dummy still has a trump, so the slam is safe in harbor.

The full deal:

	North	
	♠ Q 10 5 3 ♡ 6 ♢ Q 5 2 ♣ A K J 6 2	
♠ 8 6 4 ♡ 10 7 4 2 ♢ J 10 9 8 ♣ 10 5	N W E S	♠ 7 ♡ K J 9 5 3 ♢ K 7 6 ♣ Q 9 7 3
	♠ A K J 9 2 ♡ A Q 8 ♢ A 4 3 ♣ 8 4	

At the other table, North-South got to 6♠. They were playing weak jump shifts, so South had to respond 1♠. North raised to 2♠. South tested the water with 3♢ and North jumped to 4♡ as a splinter. South drove to slam.

West led the ♢J again: queen, king, ace. But here, South led a club to dummy and immediately returned a heart to his queen! The finesse won, so he threw a diamond from dummy on the ♡A, ruffed a heart, gave up a diamond and ruffed his last diamond in dummy.

As to the auction at our table, strong jump shifts are most useful when they suggest the possibility of slam. You don't need 19 points or any number of points. You need only to visualize a slam opposite a suitable minimum hand for your partner. Also, you should either know which suit will be trumps or bid notrump next, as I intended to do on this deal.

Suppose I had responded 1♠ and my partner had rebid 2♣. Then I would have had to grope, improvising forcing bids to try to find out more about his hand. Involving him in a slam decision would have been difficult.

9

In a club duplicate, I have a partner whose dummy play and defense are strong but whose bidding, as will be seen, is uninhibited. Neither side is vulnerable and, as South, I hold:

♠ K 8 6
♡ A K
◇ K 9 8 5 2
♣ 10 8 2

West deals and opens 1♡; my partner overcalls 2♣ and East passes. I expect to have play for 3NT opposite any kind of two-level overcall. Even:

♠ 5 4 ♡ 7 6 2 ◇ Q 3 ♣ A K 9 7 5 3

will give me a chance. There is no point in picking daisies, so I jump to 3NT, passed out. West leads the ♡Q and, when dummy hits, I see that my partner has acted in character.

Dlr: West
Vul: None

♠ A 7 4
♡ 7 5 4
◇ Q 6
♣ A J 9 6 5

♠ K 8 6
♡ A K
◇ K 9 8 5 2
♣ 10 8 2

West	North	East	South
1♡	2♣(!)	pass	3NT
all pass			

North wasn't around when they gave out fear. It's not so much that his two-level overcall on a broken five-card suit might be nailed for an 1100-point penalty — though that would be quite possible — but that I would bid too much, thinking he actually had something.

My partner must think not vulnerable means invulnerable; but overcalls at any vulnerability and level need a reason. The reason might be to compete for the partscore, look for game, obstruct the opponents' auction or direct a lead but to overcall with unclear chances of gain is just silly. North's prospects of reaching game were slim and the club suit offered limited chance of buying the contract at the partscore level.

At matchpoints, the 2♣ overcall would have been defensible if West had opened 1♢. Then, 2♣ would have had obstructive value. Over 1♡, it had less; if the opponents had a heart fit, they would already know about it.

Meanwhile, I take the ♡K and need eight more tricks before the defense can take five. West surely has one of the missing club honors — possibly both — but if I start the clubs next, leading the eight and intending to let it ride, the defense will get in and clear the hearts. I will have only eight tricks — four clubs, two hearts, two spades — and West wiFll have the ♢A as an entry to at least three good hearts.

I need a diamond trick; so, on the second trick, I lead the ♢2 through West. If his diamonds are Ax, he can beat me by rising with the ace to continue hearts. But luck is with me — and my partner — since the full deal is:

North:
♠ A 7 4
♡ 7 5 4
♢ Q 6
♣ A J 9 6 5

West:
♠ Q 3
♡ Q J 10 8 6
♢ A J 4
♣ K 7 3

East:
♠ J 10 9 5 2
♡ 9 3 2
♢ 10 7 3
♣ Q 4

South:
♠ K 8 6
♡ A K
♢ K 9 8 5 2
♣ 10 8 2

If West takes his ace, I have four diamonds, two hearts, two spades and one club. When he plays low, dummy's queen wins; I come back to my ♠K and run the ♣8. East wins and returns a heart but I can win and finesse in clubs again. I take four clubs, two hearts, two spades and one diamond.

I fear this result — our +400 scored 10 matchpoints out of 12— won't dampen my partner's enthusiasm for overcalling on a whim. But we might have reached 3NT even if he had passed. If East had also passed, I would have balanced with a double; partner might then have jumped aggressively to 3♣, inviting game, and I would have converted that to 3NT.

A tendency among some experts is to respond with sub-minimum strength to prevent the opponents from entering the auction cheaply. At a couple of tables, East responded to 1♡. At one table I heard about, East responded 1NT(!) and was marooned there. After a diamond lead and an eventual club shift, the defense took the same nine tricks that I took as declarer in 3NT. So North-South were +150 for a standoff against the pairs that won nine tricks declaring a notrump partial.

10

In a Sectional Swiss Teams, our opponents are strong. They are vulnerable, we are not and, as West, the dealer, I hold:

♠ 5
♡ J 9 8 7
♢ Q J 10 9 2
♣ 6 3 2

I know wild-eyed players who would act with my cards — they think that not being vulnerable is a license to throw discipline into the garbage can — but I cling to the old-fashioned notion that bridge is a partnership game and that your results will improve if your partner has some idea what you hold and can make informed decisions. After I pass, North opens 1♣. South jump-shifts to 2♠, North rebids 2NT, South continues with 3♡ and North gives preference to 3♠.

South then unleashes Blackwood but stops in 5♠ when North's 5♣ response shows no aces. I lead the ♢Q.

Dlr: West
Vul: N-S

North:
♠ 10 9 2
♡ K Q 6
♢ K 6 4
♣ K Q 10 5

West:
♠ 5
♡ J 9 8 7
♢ Q J 10 9 2
♣ 6 3 2

West	North	East	South
pass	1♣	pass	2♠
pass	2NT	pass	3♡
pass	3♠	pass	4NT
pass	5♣	pass	5♠
all pass			

Dummy plays low, East signals with the eight and South plays the five. With a mental shrug, I continue with the ♢10: six, three... and South ruffs with the ♠A and proceeds by cashing the ♠K and leading a club: deuce from me, king, ace. My partner leads a trump and declarer wins with the ten in dummy. He ruffs dummy's ♢K, crosses to the ♣Q and ruffs a club. South then leads to the ♡K, ruffs a club, gets back to dummy with the ♡Q and draws the missing trump with the ♠9. The ♡A wins the thirteenth trick, making five. The full deal:

West	North / South	East
	♠ 10 9 2 ♡ K Q 6 ♢ K 6 4 ♣ K Q 10 5	
♠ 5 ♡ J 9 8 7 ♢ Q J 10 9 2 ♣ 6 3 2	N W E S	♠ 8 7 3 ♡ 10 5 ♢ A 8 7 3 ♣ A J 9 8
	♠ A K Q J 6 4 ♡ A 4 3 2 ♢ 5 ♣ 7 4	

I like South's jump to 2♠, showing slam interest immediately. If South responded 1♠, North might be reluctant to cooperate in a slam hunt with a minimum such as:

♠ 10 9 2 ♡ K Q 6 ♢ 8 6 4 ♣ A K 10 5

Strong jump shifts raise the possibility of slam and enlist partner's cooperation. It's better to show interest quickly and then keep your foot on the brake than it is to start tentatively and try to catch up.

South's 3♡, though, had an unclear meaning and his 4NT was questionable. Having jumped, he should have bid 4♠ on his third turn and left any further move to North.

At the other table, sure enough, my counterpart sitting West abandoned discipline and perpetrated a weak 2♢ opening. Nothing came of that maneuver. North passed, East raised to 3♢, South came in with 3♠ and North bid 4♠, passed out. South made an overtrick and the board was pushed.

Had I defended better, we might have gained 11 IMPs. Bridge is difficult because what seems to be a normal, casual play can be costly. My diamond continuation on the second trick looked routine but gave declarer the timing to pull off a dummy reversal. (I could expect for South to have a singleton diamond; otherwise, he would not have been able to use Blackwood.)

With double-dummy play, only a club switch would beat 5♠. Say I lead a heart instead. Declarer can win with the king, draw trumps, cash the ♡A and lead a club to the king. If East takes the ace, he is endplayed; if he ducks, declarer can lead another club from dummy for the same result. A club shift on the second trick lets East win and exit safely and the defense will win another trick.

11

In a Flighted Swiss Teams, we are matched against a quartet of aspiring players. Neither side is vulnerable and, as South, I hold:

♠ A J 9 8 2
♡ A J 8 2
◇ 8
♣ Q 7 6

West, the dealer, opens 1◇, my partner passes and East raises to 2◇. I inquire and learn that 2◇ is natural and limited, not an 'inverted' raise. I come in with 2♠. A double would be a more flexible call but I would rather get my five-card suit into the game. West competes to 3◇ and my partner raises to 4♠. Everyone passes and West leads the ◇K.

Dlr: West
Vul: None

♠ Q 10 6 4 3
♡ K 7 5
◇ J 7 4
♣ K 8

♠ A J 9 8 2
♡ A J 8 2
◇ 8
♣ Q 7 6

West	North	East	South
1◇	pass	2◇	2♠
3◇	4♠	all pass	

The contract looks promising. North was light in high cards for his bid but he placed me with shortness in diamonds and his kings looked good; if I didn't hold the aces, West, who had opened the bidding, probably had them.

I have four possible losers — one in each suit — but I might be able to avoid one of them. East signals with the ◇10 and West continues with the ◇A, which I ruff. A winning finesse in either major suit will see me home. Still, West opened and may — or may not — hold at least one of the missing key honors.

I need not rush to attack the majors. Instead, I can try to place the cards. On the third trick, I lead a club to dummy's king. East produces the ace and leads the ♢Q; I ruff again. Now I'm sure that both the ♠K and ♡Q are with West; with neither honor, he might not have opened, much less bid again with at most 11 points. So I take the ♠A and both defenders follow low. Next I cash the ♣Q, ruff my last club in dummy and exit with a trump. The full deal is:

	North	
	♠ Q 10 6 4 3 ♡ K 7 5 ♢ J 7 4 ♣ K 8	
West ♠ K 5 ♡ Q 10 4 ♢ A K 9 5 2 ♣ J 9 4	N W E S	**East** ♠ 7 ♡ 9 6 3 ♢ Q 10 6 3 ♣ A 10 5 3 2
	♠ A J 9 8 2 ♡ A J 8 2 ♢ 8 ♣ Q 7 6	

When West takes the ♠K, he is endplayed, obliged to lead away from the ♡Q or concede a fatal ruff-and-sluff, and we are +420.

At the other table, my teammates were using inverted minor-suit raises. I am not an advocate of that treatment. Too many pairs agree to play inverted minors without fully discussing how the auction might develop. Moreover, some hands are neither strong nor weak and are awkward to describe.

But the treatment gains when it obstructs the opponents and that is what happened here. After 1♢-pass-3♢, the Flight B player sitting South was reluctant to come in at the three-level with such minimum high-card strength. (With diamond shortness, maybe he should have risked acting.) So, 3♢ was passed out and my team made a game at one table and a partial at the other.

12

In a Sectional Swiss Teams, we won our first match; the second was a dead tie. In the third match, the first two deals are played prosaically in 1NT — once in each direction — for +120. On the third deal, only our side is vulnerable and, as South, I hold:

♠ A Q 10 5
♡ K J 10 4 3
◇ A 2
♣ Q 4

My partner opens 1♣ and the opponents stay out. I respond 1♡ and partner raises to 2♡. Slam is possible opposite a minimum North hand:

♠ K 4 ♡ A 9 7 5 ◇ 7 6 ♣ A J 9 6 2

would be enough to give me good play for twelve tricks. I could blast into slam via Blackwood but I doubt that it will cost me to go slow. For one thing, North may have just three-card heart support; I would expect him to raise to 2♡ with:

♠ 6 3 ♡ Q 7 6 ◇ K 8 7 3 ♣ A K J 6

When I bid 2♠, partner jumps to 4♡. Now, I can reasonably either take control by bidding Blackwood or issue a further try with a 5◇ cuebid. I think that it's better for me to bid 4NT. I have made up my mind to bid a slam — Blackwood will be a formality — and if I were to cuebid 5◇ and partner huddled and signed off in 5♡, I might find myself involved in an Unauthorized Information appeal.

In response to my 4NT, my partner bids 5♡, showing two aces. (Many pairs use Keycard Blackwood; my partner and I decided to forgo it.) I bid 6♡, passed out, and West leads the ◇K.

Dlr: North	♠ 6 3 2
Vul: N-S	♡ A Q 8 5
	◊ 9 4
	♣ A K J 10
	♠ A Q 10 5
	♡ K J 10 4 3
	◊ A 2
	♣ Q 4

West	North	East	South
	1♣	pass	1♡
pass	2♡	pass	2♠
pass	4♡	pass	4NT
pass	5♡	pass	6♡
all pass			

This contract looks like a heavy favorite. I take the ◊A and then the ♡KA. West discards a diamond.

I can draw the missing trump and take two spade finesses and if East has at least one of the missing honors — about a 75% chance — I will be home. I wonder whether I can do anything if both spade honors are wrong. An endplay is possible but I'll need an extra dummy entry to eliminate the minor suits.

I can't draw the last trump. Instead, I cash three rounds of clubs. Fortunately, East follows, so I discard my diamond loser, ruff dummy's last diamond, draw the last trump with the queen, cash the fourth club for a spade discard and lead a spade to my ten. As it happens, the full deal is:

West	North / South	East
	♠ 6 3 2	
	♡ A Q 8 5	
	◊ 9 4	
	♣ A K J 10	
♠ K J 4	N	♠ 9 8 7
♡ 2	W E	♡ 9 7 6
◊ K Q 8 5 3	S	◊ J 10 7 6
♣ 9 6 3 2		♣ 8 7 5
	♠ A Q 10 5	
	♡ K J 10 4 3	
	◊ A 2	
	♣ Q 4	

West takes the ♠J but has no winning return. A spade gives me a free finesse, a diamond concedes a fatal ruff-and-sluff. So, we are +1430.

We were lucky to gain on the board. This was the other table's last board and one board had taken an age to play. North-South reached slam but South, under time pressure, looked no deeper into the play than taking two spade finesses. He went down one and we gained 17 IMPs.

Trying for my twelve tricks with an endplay was not risk-free but I think my line was best. Maybe I should have cashed only one high trump in embarking on my line. Then, if East ruffed the third club, I would be able to overruff, draw the last trump and fall back on taking two spade finesses. It looked right to take two high trumps, hoping to draw all the trumps; but it could have been wrong.

13

In a Sectional Swiss Teams, my team had a reasonable first-session score. In the first match after the break, we meet the leaders. We make an easy game on the first deal and then, with neither side vulnerable, I hold, as North:

♠ A K J 8 3
♡ Q 10 7 6
◇ J 6
♣ 7 5

My partner deals and opens 1♡; West passes.

I could force to game and if we were vulnerable, I would. If my partner had no more than:

♠ 5 4 2 ♡ A K 8 5 4 2 ◇ 8 7 ♣ A 2

game would depend on a successful finesse. But my partner has been known to open lightish. If I judge to settle for an invitation, how should I proceed? I can jump directly to 3♡ as a limit raise or I can temporize with a 1♠ response and support hearts next, perhaps with a jump-preference bid.

I could argue for either approach. A temporizing 1♠, suggesting spade length and strength, might help my partner judge whether to bid game. But if I raise directly, West will have less information to guide his opening lead and East won't be able to enter the auction at the two-level.

I toss a mental coin and respond 1♠. Partner rebids 2♡ and I stick to my plan by raising to 3♡. He goes to 4♡ and all pass. West leads the ◇K.

Dlr: South
Vul: None

♠ A K J 8 3
♡ Q 10 7 6
◇ J 6
♣ 7 5

♠ 7 6 2
♡ A K J 5 4 2
◇ A 5
♣ Q 6

West	North	East	South
			1♡
pass	1♠	pass	2♡
pass	3♡	pass	4♡
all pass			

My partner takes the ◇A and the ♡AK. The contract does appear to hang on the spade finesse and if it wins, we make at least one overtrick. But my partner spots a slight extra chance; he exits with a diamond.

West takes the queen and leads a spade; partner puts up the ace and leads a club. The full deal:

North:
♠ A K J 8 3
♡ Q 10 7 6
◇ J 6
♣ 7 5

West:
♠ 9 4
♡ 8 3
◇ K Q 10 9 4
♣ J 9 3 2

East:
♠ Q 10 5
♡ 9
◇ 8 7 3 2
♣ A K 10 8 4

South:
♠ 7 6 2
♡ A K J 5 4 2
◇ A 5
♣ Q 6

East cashes the ♣K and ♣A but is endplayed. Well done, partner! His good play deserved to gain us 10 IMPs — and did when 4♡ went down in the replay.

In a Two-over-One system where a two-level response is forcing to game, a responder with invitational values cannot temporize by bidding a new suit at the two-level. He has to fall back on a murky forcing 1NT response.

In another of my books, I presented this scenario. You hold:

♠ A K Q 9 7
♡ A 6 4 2
◇ 6
♣ Q 6 5

You open 1♠, partner responds 1NT (forcing), you bid 2♡ and he jumps to 3♠ to invite you to game.

You bid 4♠? Too bad. The hands are:

West		East
♠ A K Q 9 7	N	♠ J 10 4
♡ A 6 4 2	W E	♡ Q 7 3
◇ 6	S	◇ A K 8 4
♣ Q 6 5		♣ 7 4 2

The opening lead is a club and they cash three clubs. The ♡K is wrong as well and you go down two.

You pass 3♠? Too bad. The hands are:

West		East
♠ A K Q 9 7	N	♠ J 10 4
♡ A 6 4 2	W E	♡ Q 7 3
◇ 6	S	◇ 7 4 2
♣ Q 6 5		♣ A K 8 4

The ♡K is wrong again but you still win ten tricks.

If responder can temporize with an old-fashioned 2♣ response on the second hand, opener will be encouraged to bid game. Not so, though, if responder has suggested diamond strength. The question is whether such auctions help the defenders more than they help you. In my opinion, they don't; this is shown again in the following deal.

14

In a Sectional Swiss Teams, we won a blitz in our first match. On the first deal of the second match, our opponents bid and made a routine game. Then, with only our side vulnerable, I, as South, hold:

♠ A J 6 5 2
♡ A K Q 4
◇ 7 3
♣ 10 4

East, the dealer, passes; I open 1♠. West passes and my partner raises to 3♠. My idea of a limit raise is a hand with prime values and good distribution but limited high-card strength and without concentrated side-suit values. I would raise to 3♠ with:

♠K 10 4 3 ♡2 ◇A J 5 4 ♣7 6 5 3

But if I held:

♠Q 10 4 3 ♡3 2 ◇7 6 5 ♣A K J 5

I would (using Standard methods) temporize with a 2♣ response and support spades at the minimum level next.

That style is exceedingly old-fashioned, and would be impossible in the Two-over-One approach, but it isn't necessarily ineffective. If my partner can infer the location of my side strength, it may help him to judge the auction accurately. Of course, the defenders may be helped too; but in my opinion, that is a lesser consideration.

I must decide whether to bid game. I have four minor-suit losers and my trumps are nothing special but the vulnerable-game bonus is seductive, so I bid 4♠ and hope I will have some play for it. All pass and West leads the ♣2.

Dlr: East
Vul: N-S

♠ K 10 4 3
♡ 6 3
◇ A Q 5 2
♣ J 7 3

♠ A J 6 5 2
♡ A K Q 4
◇ 7 3
♣ 10 4

West	North	East	South
		pass	1♠
pass	3♠	pass	4♠
all pass			

This is a good contract. I need to pick up the trumps or find the ◇K with West. East takes the ♣K and ♣A and continues with a low club; I ruff.

I don't have a clue about how the trumps lie but if I misguess and lose to the queen, I will go down if the diamond finesse fails. But wait. If East has the ◇K, he won't have the ♠Q. With a hand such as:

♠Q 9 7 ♡10 9 2 ◇K 10 8 ♣A K 9 5

most Easts would have opened the bidding, especially at favorable vulnerability.

Acting on my hypothetical view of the deal, I take the ♠A and lead a second trump; when West follows low, I play dummy's ten. The full deal happens to be:

West	North	East
	♠ K 10 4 3 ♡ 6 3 ◇ A Q 5 2 ♣ J 7 3	
♠ Q 8 7 ♡ J 7 2 ◇ J 9 6 ♣ Q 8 6 2	N / W E / S	♠ 9 ♡ 10 9 8 5 ◇ K 10 8 4 ♣ A K 9 5
	♠ A J 6 5 2 ♡ A K Q 4 ◇ 7 3 ♣ 10 4	

Making four.

At the other table, South judged to pass North's raise to 3♠. He was +140, misguessing in trumps and losing a diamond, and may have been pleased with that result.

The odds favor bidding close vulnerable games, especially in a long match. If I had gone down at 4♠, we would have lost 6 IMPs. As it was, we gained 10.

As to the play, I made what Terence Reese called a 'second-degree assumption'. You assume that a certain card lies so that the contract is safe or at risk, and then you follow the consequences of your assumption to place other vital cards. If my trump finesse had lost to East's doubleton queen, I could expect to make the contract anyway because I could assume that the diamond finesse would win. Alternatively, I might have taken the diamond finesse early to get a clue about the location of the ♠Q.

15

The role of memory — long-term and short-term — in bridge reminds me of the sweet elderly couple who had taken a course to improve their memory. The husband was trying to recall the instructor's name.

"What's that flower," he muttered, "with thorns and a sweet smell?"

"A rose?" someone prompted him.

"That's it," he said, looking at his wife. "Rose, who was the instructor for that memory course?"

In a local teams event, North-South are vulnerable and I am East with:

♠ Q 5 3 2
♡ 8 6 5
◇ A Q 4
♣ Q 8 7

South deals and opens 1♣; my partner and I never enter the auction. North responds 1♠, South rebids 1NT, North raises to 2NT and South goes on to 3NT. Everyone passes and my partner leads the ♡Q.

Dlr: South
Vul: N-S

North:
♠ A K J 10
♡ 4 3
◇ J 9 6
♣ J 6 5 3

East:
♠ Q 5 3 2
♡ 8 6 5
◇ A Q 4
♣ Q 8 7

West	North	East	South
			1♣
pass	1♠	pass	1NT
pass	2NT	pass	3NT
all pass			

North's raise to 2NT was hungry — some would say famished. At IMPs, the odds favor bidding aggressive vulnerable games. Suppose you bid 4♠ and make it for +620 and in the replay, your opponents stop in 3♠ for

+170. You gain 10 IMPs. Now say that you go down in 4♠ for -100 when they are +140. You lose 6 IMPs. So you figure to gain by bidding a game that has about a 40% chance.

Those odds assume that you won't go down more than one and won't be doubled. They also apply over the course of many deals. If you played a one-deal match, they wouldn't matter and they only matter in a limited way in a short Swiss match.

I follow with the ♡5 and declarer wins with the king. He cashes the ♣A and leads a spade: seven, ace. He returns a club to his ten and West follows low. Then comes a second spade: six, jack — and I take the queen.

If West led from AQJ10x in hearts, I can beat the contract with a heart return (or with any return, in fact, since declarer will only have eight tricks to cash). But with that hand, West might have acted over South's 1♣. Moreover, I do remember that South accepted North's game invitation, so I can assume that South has a little extra strength. I doubt that he would accept with:

♠ 9 8 4 ♡ K 9 7 ◇ K 7 2 ♣ A K 10 9

so I lead the ◇A. West encourages with the eight and I continue with the queen and a third diamond — beating the contract since the full deal is:

West		East
	North ♠ A K J 10 ♡ 4 3 ◇ J 9 6 ♣ J 6 5 3	
♠ 7 6 ♡ Q J 10 9 2 ◇ K 8 5 3 ♣ 4 2	N W E S	♠ Q 5 3 2 ♡ 8 6 5 ◇ A Q 4 ♣ Q 8 7
	South ♠ 9 8 4 ♡ A K 7 ◇ 10 7 2 ♣ A K 10 9	

At the other table, the bidding started the same way but North passed 1NT, despite being vulnerable. Regardless of the game-bidding odds, to raise with that North hand wouldn't occur to me. My teammates were +120 and we gained 6 IMPs.

In retrospect, I wonder whether South might have accepted a game try with the hand I had assumed he wouldn't hold, such as:

♠ 9 8 4 ♡ K 9 7 ◇ K 7 2 ♣ A K 10 9

Partnerships should have an agreement about bidding vulnerable games. You can stretch to invite — the approach I prefer, lest good games be missed — or you can invite soundly and stretch to accept — an approach that may mean you avoid going down in your try. But if both players stretch, hopeless games will result.

16

In a local Swiss Teams, we are playing the last match to win the event. On the first deal, both sides are vulnerable and, as South, the dealer, I pick up:

♠ A K J 6 2
♡ A Q 6 2
◇ Q 9 2
♣ J

I open 1♠ and my partner raises to 2♠. The opponents contribute green cards. Since we are vulnerable, I could just blast into 4♠. Even if the contract isn't cold, good defense might be needed to beat it and the opening leader will know nothing about my hand except that I was willing to bid game over a single raise.

Expert pairs are aggressive in bidding vulnerable games but if both partners stretch, hopeless games will result. As discussed in the previous deal, one might go one of two ways here. One approach is to stretch to invite; with a sound invitation, you just bid game and hope for the best. The alternative is to invite soundly; that approach reduces the chance of going down in your try. My preference is the first approach, lest good games be missed, but I believe the majority of experts embrace the second.

What I should do with this hand isn't clear; but I would hate to bid 4♠ and see dummy hit with:

♠Q 5 4 ♡5 4 3 ◇J 6 ♣K 7 6 5 2

If I'm going to settle for a try, bidding 3♡ is best. Help in hearts will be useful, and if partner's hand is:

♠5 4 3 ♡K 8 5 4 3 ◇A 6 ♣6 5 2

a contract of 4♡ will be superior.

Over my 3♡, he jumps to 4♠ and everyone passes. West huddles and leads the ♡J.

Dlr; South
Vul: Both

♠ 10 5 4 3
♡ K 5
◇ 6 5
♣ K Q 6 5 2

♠ A K J 6 2
♡ A Q 6 2
◇ Q 9 2
♣ J

West	North	East	South
			1♠
pass	2♠	pass	3♡
pass	4♠	all pass	

My partner certainly has his bid. If his hand had been a little better, he would have been worth a limit raise to 3♠. But 4♠ isn't laydown, even with this friendly lead.

Suppose I take the ♡K and cash the ♠AK. All will be well if the queen falls: I will have five trump tricks, three hearts, at least one club and at least one ruff in dummy and I will have at most two top losers. But if a defender has Qxx in trumps, I could be in trouble. I might need two ruffs in dummy and I might not be able to prevent the defender with the ♠Q from getting in to draw one of dummy's trumps.

So, I take just the ♠A and then the ♡AQ, pitching one of dummy's diamond losers. Both defenders follow, West with the seven and ten. Next, I lead the ♣J. East shrugs and takes the ace. He shifts to a diamond and West wins with the jack and returns a low diamond. I ruff in dummy, discard my last heart on the ♣K, lead a trump and put up the king when East follows low. West discards but I ruff my last diamond in dummy. East gets just the master ♠Q and I make the contract. The full deal:

	North	
	♠ 10 5 4 3 ♡ K 5 ◇ 6 5 ♣ K Q 6 5 2	
West ♠ 7 ♡ J 10 7 ◇ A J 7 4 3 ♣ 8 7 4 3	N W E S	**East** ♠ Q 9 8 ♡ 9 8 4 3 ◇ K 10 8 ♣ A 10 9
	South ♠ A K J 6 2 ♡ A Q 6 2 ◇ Q 9 2 ♣ J	

At the other table, the contract and opening lead were the same but after South won the first heart, he took the AK of trumps. When West discarded, declarer continued with the ♡AQ for a diamond discard.

South then led the ♣J, West signaled count with the eight and my teammate in East found the winning play of ducking. He lost his ♣A but the trick came back with 100% interest because declarer was deprived of the two winners in dummy.

Declarer continued with his fourth heart. If West had followed, declarer could have succeeded by pitching dummy's last diamond as a loser-on-loser. As it was, East was sure to get in and take his ♠Q, leaving declarer a trick short of his goal.

17

In the first match after the dinner break in a Sectional Swiss Teams, the first three boards have been mundane. On the fourth, both sides are vulnerable and, as South, I hold:

♠ A K Q J
♡ J 9 8 2
◇ A J 10
♣ 6 3

Three passes to me. For a second, I am tempted to open 1♠, or to open 1◇ and hope for a major-suit response, but either call would be a case of masterminding. I open 1NT, preferring the bid that best describes my hand. My partner raises to 3NT and everyone passes. West leads the ♡5 and North stoically puts down his dummy.

Dlr: West
Vul: Both

♠ 6 4
♡ 7 3
◇ 8 7 4
♣ A K 8 7 4 2

♠ A K Q J
♡ J 9 8 2
◇ A J 10
♣ 6 3

West	North	East	South
pass	pass	pass	1NT
pass	3NT	all pass	

This looks grim. Even if the defenders don't run four or five hearts, I have just seven top tricks. My partner's bid was hungry; some would say famished. As I have mentioned before, the odds favor bidding speculative vulnerable games at IMPs, and North was loath to miss one. He hoped his clubs would run. Still, in an eight-board match, the odds don't have much time to take effect. (In a one-board match, you would just need to make a winning decision in a game-or-partscore situation.)

East wins the first heart with the queen and returns the ten. I cover gratefully with the jack, and West takes the king and ace and leads a fourth heart to my eight, as East pitches a spade.

Now what? I'm up to eight winners, and I can get another if the clubs break 3-2, ducking a club to keep a link with dummy. The alternative is to use the high clubs as entries to take two finesses in diamonds.

On percentage, to attack the diamonds is correct. East will have at least one of the missing honors about three-quarters of the time and a 3-2 club break is only about a 68% chance. But it occurs to me that a diamond play is all but a sure thing: West passed as dealer and has shown the ♡AK, so he won't have the ◇KQ (and perhaps a club honor) as well. So I lead a club to dummy and return a diamond to my jack. West wins with the queen and leads a spade, and I win, go back to the other high club and lead a diamond to my ten. We are +600, as the full deal is:

West	North / South	East
	♠ 6 4 ♡ 7 3 ◇ 8 7 4 ♣ A K 8 7 4 2	
♠ 9 8 5 3 ♡ A K 6 5 ◇ Q 9 6 3 ♣ 10	N W E S	♠ 10 7 2 ♡ Q 10 4 ◇ K 5 2 ♣ Q J 9 5
	♠ A K Q J ♡ J 9 8 2 ◇ A J 10 ♣ 6 3	

At the other table, North-South reached an unexpected contract. There, it was the last deal of the match and South must not have liked the way things were going. After three passes, he tried to create a swing by opening 1♠, treating his robust suit as a five-carder. When North responded 1NT, South rebid 2♡ and North took a 2♠ preference. South might have acted again but he had no obvious source of tricks. On a diamond lead, he managed eight tricks in 2♠ for +110. I have to admit that the 2♠ contract was not much worse than our 3NT but we gained 10 IMPs anyway.

South's attempt to stir up the pot struck me as questionable. He may have thought his team was behind; but a player should always assume that his teammates are having a winning set.

18

In the first match after the dinner break in a Sectional Swiss Teams, we are playing a capable team. Only our side is vulnerable and, as South, I hold:

♠ Q J 10 9 5
♡ 9 6 3
◇ A Q 5
♣ 10 5

West, the dealer, opens 3♣; my partner doubles and East enterprisingly puts it up to 5♣.

I have to take a position; this deal belongs to us, so I must double or bid. In a long match, I might double and settle for a reasonable result. If my partner has an average hand for his three-level double, I can expect to beat 5♣ doubled by two tricks, maybe three. But remember that if I were playing in a one-board match, I would just have to guess right and a seven-board Swiss match is somewhat similar. If the other six boards are uneventful, this board may decide the match.

I hate to let the opponents push me around but we may even have a slam, and then collecting +300 against 5♣ doubled might mean a big adverse swing. So, I bid 5♠, expecting to have play for eleven tricks. Everyone passes. The opponents are satisfied to have pushed us to the five-level, where they have a better chance of beating us. West leads the ♣K.

Dlr: West
Vul: N-S

♠ A K 7 3
♡ K Q J
◇ J 7 6 3 2
♣ 7

♠ Q J 10 9 5
♡ 9 6 3
◇ A Q 5
♣ 10 5

West	North	East	South
3♣	dbl	5♣	5♠
all pass			

That's a skinny dummy with only 14 points in high cards. The shape is attractive and I guess most players would have doubled; but I would have preferred a bit more strength. Since both North and I were aggressive, 5♠ is an underdog.

On the second trick, West leads a heart and East takes the ace and returns a heart. West follows, so I'm not down yet. I draw trumps; they break 2-2. (That's two tricks West would have lost in 5♣ doubled.) When I cash my last heart winner, postponing the evil moment in diamonds, West follows. (That's two more.)

My normal play in diamonds is low to the queen but that cannot be right here. West started with two spades, at least three hearts and probably seven clubs. Even if he only had six clubs, there isn't room in his hand for three diamonds and if East has, say, K109, he will always win a diamond trick.

As the only chance, I bang down the ♢A and it happens to be my lucky day. The full deal is:

	♠ A K 7 3 ♡ K Q J ♢ J 7 6 3 2 ♣ 7	
♠ 8 4 ♡ 8 7 4 ♢ K ♣ K Q J 9 6 4 3	N W E S	♠ 6 2 ♡ A 10 5 2 ♢ 10 9 8 4 ♣ A 8 2
	♠ Q J 10 9 5 ♡ 9 6 3 ♢ A Q 5 ♣ 10 5	

Making five, +650.

At the other table, West opened 3♣ again but North wanted more to act and passed. Then, my teammate in East came up with the excellent tactical bid of 3NT. South and West passed and, though North might have suspected that he was being robbed, he passed too.

South led the ♠Q and the defense took five spades and three diamonds before declarer got in. The result was down four, +200 to North-South, but my team gained 10 IMPs. My partner and I couldn't take credit for it, since our result was lucky. Next time, I shall double 5♣ for +500 and settle for a smaller gain.

19

In a Sectional Swiss Teams, we are playing the penultimate match against an all-expert team. With both sides vulnerable, I hold, as South:

♠ A K 7
♡ 10 8
◇ K 9 4
♣ J 10 9 8 3

We have the auction to ourselves. North, the dealer, opens 1◇ and I respond 2♣, not forcing to game in our style. North raises to 3♣ and I bid 3◇. He tries 3♡.

I guess I could bid 3NT but I'm nervous about it. After the certain spade opening lead, I will probably have to go after the clubs and my jack-high suit may take time to establish. Instead of committing us to notrump, I bid 3♠, which I hope partner will treat as showing spade strength but uncertainty.

He thinks it over and jumps to 5♣; everyone passes. I hope my 3♠ wasn't a transfer — shifting the blame to partner if I go down in 5♣ when 3NT would have made. West leads the ♡6.

Dlr: North
Vul: Both

North:
♠ 4
♡ A K J 9
◇ Q J 10 5
♣ K 7 6 4

South:
♠ A K 7
♡ 10 8
◇ K 9 4
♣ J 10 9 8 3

West	North	East	South
	1◇	pass	2♣
pass	3♣	pass	3◇
pass	3♡	pass	3♠
pass	5♣	all pass	

North's bidding was reasonable. I don't mind being in a vulnerable game that seems to depend on a winning finesse. I take the ♡A, cross back with a high spade and lead the ♣J: deuce, four, ace. Now I look like a favorite — unless that heart lead was a singleton. But East thinks for a long time. Finally, he tables... the ♡Q.

I win in dummy but if West still has ♣Q5, I have to get to my hand to repeat the finesse. Ruffing a heart clearly risks an overruff. I can try a diamond but if East has the ace, he will rise and lead a third heart. Should I just take the ♣K and hope the queen falls?

As it happens, I have no winning play. The full deal is:

West	North / South	East
	♠ 4 ♡ A K J 9 ♢ Q J 10 5 ♣ K 7 6 4	
♠ J 9 8 6 2 ♡ 6 4 ♢ 8 7 2 ♣ Q 5 2	N W E S	♠ Q 10 5 3 ♡ Q 7 5 3 2 ♢ A 6 3 ♣ A
	♠ A K 7 ♡ 10 8 ♢ K 9 4 ♣ J 10 9 8 3	

When I judge to call for a diamond, East grabs his ace and leads a third heart and I go down when West scores his ♣Q.

My partner and I compliment East. We can appreciate a fine defensive play, even when it costs us a game. If East leads anything but the ♡Q on the fourth trick, I can get to my hand and pick up the trumps, losing only two tricks for +600.

Bridge can be a cruel game. At the other table, North-South played in 3NT and the opening lead was a spade. The expert South won and made an uncharacteristic error when he let the ♣J ride next. He failed to note that even if the club finesse won, he had only eight tricks and would need a third heart trick. He should instead have forced out the ♢A, intending to finesse in hearts and hoping for four hearts, three diamonds and two spades.

When East took the ♣A and returned a spade, South realized his miscalculation. He took four club tricks and let the ♡10 ride. East produced the queen and the defense ran the spades for down two. So the East at my table still lost 3 IMPs after his good defense. At least he could tell himself that he didn't lose 13.

20

Entering the last round of a club duplicate, I estimate that we need two good results to win or come close.

I personally dislike the feature on electronic scoring devices that reveals your percentage result on a deal. It's a distraction and can cause delay. It damages the integrity of the game when pairs who know that they are doing poorly are motivated to 'swing' — take wild chances to catch up. It may lead to a remark that, even if not intended as such, could be regarded as gloating. For me, judging how well you are doing is part of the game.

Only the opponents are vulnerable and, as South, I hold:

♠ A K J 10 9 8 7
♡ 9 8 6 2
◇ –
♣ 10 5

My partner deals and opens 1◇, I respond 1♠, he rebids 2◇ and I jump to 4♠. I might not make it. I'm overbidding my high cards and I have a bunch of losers... but I can't imagine getting a top by staying out of game with this hand.

My partner huddles... and bids 6♠. Maybe he has the same ideas about trying for a top as I do. Everyone passes and West leads the ♣K.

Dlr: North
Vul: E-W

♠ Q 2
♡ A K 5 4
◇ A J 9 6 5 2
♣ 3

♠ A K J 10 9 8 7
♡ 9 8 6 2
◇ –
♣ 10 5

West	North	East	South
	1◇	pass	1♠
pass	2◇	pass	4♠
pass	6♠	all pass	

"You didn't jump to 4♠ directly over 1♢," my partner remarks, "so I assume you have a decent hand."

I suppose he has a point. My 4♠ was an overbid. If this slam fails, the fault will be mine.

On the second trick, West shifts to a trump. I can count eleven tricks: seven spades, a club ruff in dummy, two hearts and a diamond. If the diamonds break well, I can establish my 12th trick in that suit. So I take the ♠Q, discard a heart on the ♢A, ruff a diamond, ruff a club in dummy — East follows with the jack — and ruff a diamond.

West discards a club, so that's the end of me scoring a long diamond: I'm one dummy entry short for that. I still have a chance if East has heart length as well as his diamond length: I cash some more trumps, discarding two hearts from dummy. As I hope, the position after nine tricks is

	♠ — ♡ A K ♢ J 9 ♣ —	
♠ — ♡ 10 ♢ — ♣ Q 9 8	N W E S	♠ — ♡ Q J 7 ♢ K Q ♣ —
	♠ 7 ♡ 9 8 6 ♢ — ♣ —	

East, still to discard, can't cope. If he throws a diamond, I can lead a heart to dummy and ruff a diamond and then dummy is high. When East discards a heart, I take the ♡AK and my hand is high. The full deal:

♠ Q 2
♡ A K 5 4
◇ A J 9 6 5 2
♣ 3

♠ 5 4 3	N	♠ 6
♡ 10	W E	♡ Q J 7 3
◇ 8 4	S	◇ K Q 10 7 3
♣ K Q 9 8 6 4 2		♣ A J 7

♠ A K J 10 9 8 7
♡ 9 8 6 2
◇ —
♣ 10 5

West could have beaten 6♠ by shifting to a heart at trick two, removing a vital entry from dummy, but it was hard for him to foresee a trump squeeze. He imagined that I might have a third club I needed to ruff in dummy. More reasonably, West might have chosen a trump opening lead.

Our +980 was indeed worth 11 1/2 matchpoints out of 12 but, as is often the case, we risked a lot to gain little. If we had played in 4♠, avoided best defense and scored +480, we would have scored 11. Bidding a borderline game or slam at matchpoints is questionable. If you need good luck or good play to make it, you can expect a good matchpoint result just for winning the maximum number of tricks.

21

In a Regional Knockout Teams, with neither side vulnerable, as South, I hold:

♠ —
♡ A K J 9 8 5
◇ 8 7 3
♣ K J 7 3

West, the dealer, passes, my partner opens 1◇, East overcalls 1♠, I bid 2♡ and West competes with 2♠. My partner huddles, consults the ceiling and produces a gentle raise to 6♡. East passes.

Partner may be gambling a bit but he can't know that I have a sixth heart. He may suspect I have a spade void but he couldn't have known for sure. I really have no right to take the push to seven since I can't count thirteen tricks but I can't believe I won't have a play for it.

You only live once, so I bid 7♡ and everyone passes. West leads the ♠7 and I await the dummy edgily.

"I could have had more," my partner says — not quite what I want to hear.

Dlr: West
Vul: None

♠ Q 10 6 3
♡ Q 10 6 3
◇ A K 5 4
♣ A

♠ —
♡ A K J 9 8 5
◇ 8 7 3
♣ K J 7 3

West	North	East	South
pass	1◇	1♠	2♡
2♠	6♡	pass	7♡
all pass			

I suppose he could have had a bit more; even the ◇J in addition might have made a difference. But I can't fault his bid, since we would have had good play for 6♡ even if I had held a dead-minimum hand such as:

♠ 2 ♡ A K 9 8 5 ◇ Q J 3 ♣ 9 8 7 6

I seem to have gotten us into a losing grand slam. Maybe I should have been disciplined instead of speculative. Dummy plays the ten on the first spade, East produces the jack and I ruff. The contract isn't hopeless. If the ♣Q is doubleton or tripleton and the trumps break 2-1, I can get two diamond pitches from dummy and ruff a diamond for the thirteenth trick. So, I lead to the ♣A, return a trump to my hand (East-West follow), take the ♣K, discarding a diamond from dummy, and ruff a third club high.

East discards a spade, so I can forget about scoring the ♣J. But it seems that East has length in diamonds as well as in spades, so hope remains. I ruff a spade, ruff the ♣J high and take two more trumps, pitching dummy's last low diamond.

With four tricks to go, I'm hoping the position is:

	North ♠ Q 10 ♡ — ◇ A K ♣ —	
♠ K ♡ — ◇ 10 6 ♣ Q	N W E S	♠ A 9 ♡ — ◇ Q J 9 ♣ —
	South ♠ — ♡ A ◇ 8 7 3 ♣ —	

Sure enough, East still has a discard to make and can't hold the fort. If he throws a spade, I lead a diamond to dummy and ruff a spade; dummy is high. When East actually throws a diamond, I take the ◇AK and my hand is high.

A trump squeeze has come to my rescue and we are +1510. The full deal:

	♠ Q 10 6 3 ♡ Q 10 6 3 ◇ A K 5 4 ♣ A	
West ♠ K 8 7 ♡ 7 2 ◇ 10 6 ♣ Q 10 9 6 5 2	N W E S	**East** ♠ A J 9 5 4 2 ♡ 4 ◇ Q J 9 2 ♣ 8 4
	♠ — ♡ A K J 9 8 5 ◇ 8 7 3 ♣ K J 7 3	

The result at the other table made my 7♡ adventure look silly. There, North opened 1◇ and my teammate in East jumped to 2♠, preemptive. South bid 3♡ and West passed. North couldn't think of an intelligent way to try for slam and, for all he knew, South could have held:

♠ J 5 ♡ A J 8 7 2 ◇ J 3 ♣ K Q 7 3

and 5♡ would be in jeopardy. So North settled for a raise to 4♡.

Though South might well have tried for slam with a 4♠ cuebid, North could have held:

♠ A J 2 ♡ 7 4 2 ◇ A Q 5 4 ♣ Q 4 2

So, silence followed and North-South were +510. Losing contracts often result when both players take reasonable but slightly conservative positions.

Bidding speculative grand slams is against the odds — in more ways than one. As it turned out, we would have gained 11 IMPs for playing in 6♡, +1010. Our grand slam gained us only 3 IMPs more and would have lost 11 had it failed.

22

In a matchpoint event, your fate depends not solely on how well you play but on how well your opponents play. If they make no errors, your chances of winning are nil. This is a deal from a Flight A Pairs in which we fell into a good result because our opponent was a thoughtful player.

You can view the problem as declarer.

Dlr: South	♠ A K Q 6
Vul: N-S	♡ 7 4
	◇ J 7 6 3
	♣ 8 5 2
	♠ 9
	♡ A K
	◇ Q 10 8 5 2
	♣ A Q 7 4 3

West	North	East	South
			1◇
pass	1♠	pass	2♣
pass	3◇	pass	3NT
all pass			

North's jump-preference to 3◇ was game-invitational. West leads the ♡3: four, ten, king. How should declarer play 3NT?

Declarer thought for a while and then led a diamond. West played low and, as East, I took the king and returned a heart. Declarer won and led another diamond. West won and cashed three hearts for down one. The full deal:

	♠ A K Q 6 ♡ 7 4 ♢ J 7 6 3 ♣ 8 5 2	
♠ 10 8 7 ♡ Q 9 8 3 2 ♢ A 9 4 ♣ J 9	N W E S	♠ J 5 4 3 2 ♡ J 10 6 5 ♢ K ♣ K 10 6
	♠ 9 ♡ A K ♢ Q 10 8 5 2 ♣ A Q 7 4 3	

North was displeased.

"What are you doing?" he asked South incredulously. "Lead a low club on Trick 2. Win the heart return, cash dummy's high spades and finesse with the ♣Q. You take four clubs, two hearts and three spades."

"I would need clubs to break 3-2 with the king onside," South pointed out. "That's only a 34% chance. If the club finesse had lost, I would be down at least three. My play ensured I could be no worse than down one."

One aspect of matchpoint dummy play is assessing your contract. If the contract is 'normal' — one that every pair in the game will reach — whether you make it is not the issue. What matters is how many tricks you take. In an 'abnormal' contract — say, a doubled partscore — you would need to play safe to guarantee making it. At IMPs, of course, you focus on making what you have bid.

Was South's 3NT a normal spot? I suppose it was. North-South had 25 high-card points, a source of tricks and all suits under control. Some pairs might reach 5♢, down at least one. If South judged that every North-South would reach 3NT, he would come out ahead, in theory, by settling for down one.

As it happened, our matchpoint score was 9 out of a possible 12. A few North-Souths played in a diamond partial for +130. A few others reached and made 3NT; those declarers were apparently unconcerned about extra undertricks.

I sympathized with our declarer. Still, there is a theory that one should never play for a minus score at matchpoints. You can decide for yourself whether that is valid.

23

In a Sectional Stratified Pairs, our opponents are experienced and my partner is scientific. He has embraced the idea that every double has some arcane meaning — and I can't dissuade him of it.

With neither side vulnerable, he deals as South and opens 1NT. West passes and I, as North, hold:

♠ A 6
♡ K 9 7 5 2
◇ A Q
♣ Q J 10 3

Clearly, we could have a slam on. South may have a heart fit or a club fit or a maximum 1NT opening. I start with 2◇, a transfer to hearts. After partner accepts the transfer, I plan to bid 3♣ and see how he reacts. (Most pairs treat a new-suit bid after a transfer as forcing and that is our agreement. My personal feeling is that an invitational meaning is better.)

I don't get to execute my plan, since East preempts with 3♠. Two passes follow. I could continue with 4♣ but I see no reason not to double. Slam is uncertain, especially when the preempt increases the chance of bad breaks, and we will surely have a chance of beating this by at least three tricks for +500: more than the value of a game.

When I double, my partner huddles. I know what is coming and, sure enough, he... bids 4◇. Did he think my double was for takeout?

I am tempted to leap to 6NT out of frustration but I have to deal with the situation properly. I can't bid 4NT; he would pass without a thought and slam is still possible. I try cuebidding 4♠... and he jumps to 6◇! Oh my. He thinks my cuebid agreed diamonds. I wish I had signed off in 4NT after all.

I suppose he might have a chunky five- or even six-card diamond suit; 6◇ might even be the double-dummy spot. So I pass; then, East doubles. I know what that means. He has a void in hearts or clubs and is asking West to find a killer lead. After two more passes, I run to 6NT and all pass. What a trial this auction has been.

West leads the ♠3.

Dlr: South
Vul: None

♠ A 6
♡ K 9 7 5 2
◇ A Q
♣ Q J 10 3

♠ J 5 2
♡ A 8 3
◇ K J 9 4
♣ A K 5

West	North	East	South
			1NT
pass	2◇	3♠	pass
pass	dbl	pass	4◇(!)
pass	4♠	pass	6◇(!)
pass	pass	dbl	pass
pass	6NT	all pass	

My partner gives dummy a sour look. He calls for the ♠A, then takes the ♡AK — both defenders follow — and leads a third heart. If West wins, we are safe for twelve tricks. But disaster comes calling: East produces the ♡Q and runs the spades for down six.

"Down one?" my partner asks when he finally claims the rest. At least he has a sense of humor. I say nothing. Some results are too grim for words. The full deal:

North:
♠ A 6
♡ K 9 7 5 2
◇ A Q
♣ Q J 10 3

West:
♠ 3
♡ J 6
◇ 10 8 7 6
♣ 9 8 7 6 4 2

East:
♠ K Q 10 9 8 7 4
♡ Q 10 4
◇ 5 3 2
♣ —

South:
♠ J 5 2
♡ A 8 3
◇ K J 9 4
♣ A K 5

East's 'Lightner' double of 6♢ was wrong in theory: 6♢ would have failed even on a spade lead and my partner could have made 6NT. He can take the ♠A and ♢AQ and lead a club to his ace. When East discards a spade, South cashes the ♢KJ. Then, placing East with 7-3-3-0 shape, he could take three more clubs. After nine tricks, East would have to save his three hearts and bare his ♠K. Then declarer could lead a spade, and his jack would provide the twelfth trick.

If, instead, East had shown length in the minor suits, declarer could have placed West with heart length and tried the hearts.

I didn't tell my partner what I thought of his 4♢ bid but he had well and truly lost his mind. Even a noted theoretician such as Eric Kokish, who is unhappy when he can't double for takeout, 'action' or a weather report, would have passed my double of 3♠. But I fear that in twenty years' time, penalty doubles will be extinct.

At matchpoints, we would have done better to stay out of slam after East's preempt. If we play in 4NT and my partner manages twelve tricks for +490, we get a near-top. Bidding slams is fun; but if (as I have stated elsewhere) making slam requires good play or luck, you will score well whether you bid it or not. If you go down, you get a bottom.

24

In a local club duplicate, I have a partner who never met a hand he didn't like. I've had my foot on the brake pedal all day, trying to compensate for his aggressive bidding.

On the next-to-last round, both sides are vulnerable and, as South, I deal and hold:

♠ A Q J 10 2
♡ A 6 3
◇ 2
♣ K Q 10 2

I open 1♠ and my partner responds 2◇, which is not forcing to game but might as well be with him. I bid 3♣. I don't like my singleton diamond and I wish I had another high-card point or two for my three-level reverse; but I do have a couple of tens and no other action is attractive.

Partner returns to 3♠. That's forcing when we have both shown strength and I suppose I need to show my ♡A next, in case he is aspiring to slam. When I cuebid 4♡, partner wheels out a 4NT Keycard inquiry. (I am not a devotee of RKC Blackwood; I agree with Edgar Kaplan, who insisted that the king of trumps is not an ace, no matter what anybody says, and pretending it is can cause trouble. But my partner insisted on it.) I bid 5♠, showing two keycards and the ♠Q, and he goes to 6♠. Everyone passes and West leads a trump.

Dlr: South
Vul: Both

North:
♠ K 8 5
♡ J 9 4
◇ A J 5 3
♣ A 6 5

South:
♠ A Q J 10 2
♡ A 6 3
◇ 2
♣ K Q 10 2

West	North	East	South
			1♠
pass	2◇	pass	3♣
pass	3♠	pass	4♡
pass	4NT	pass	5♠
pass	6♠	all pass	

My partner's bidding was as bold as ever but this poor slam is more my fault. After I showed extra values with 3♣, I should simply have bid 4♠ over his 3♠. My partner was entitled to think my 4♡ showed slam interest; I shouldn't have encouraged him. It's easy enough to say that 4♡ was free and promised no extra strength but it's human nature for partners to bid aggressively when they hear a cuebid. A style in which cuebids below game are 'obligatory' compromises the main advantage of cuebidding: to let either partner use judgment.

Is there any way to take twelve tricks? If the clubs produce four tricks, I have eleven in all. An unlikely lie of the hearts would give me a second heart trick and I can see one slight additional chance. To start with, I win the first trump in my hand and lead a low heart. West plays low and dummy's nine loses to East's queen. Back comes a second trump; I win in my hand and West follows.

I cash the ♡A next and both defenders play low. Now I'm down to hoping for a miracle but I take the ♣KA and lead a third club from dummy. When East follows low, I finesse with the ten. And lo, the full deal is:

West	North	East
	♠ K 8 5	
	♡ J 9 4	
	◇ A J 5 3	
	♣ A 6 5	
♠ 6 4	N	♠ 9 7 3
♡ K 10 5 2	W E	♡ Q 8 7
◇ K 10 8 6 4	S	◇ A 9 7
♣ 7 4		♣ J 9 8 3
	♠ A Q J 10 2	
	♡ A 6 3	
	◇ 2	
	♣ K Q 10 2	

When West throws a diamond, I take the ♣Q and discard dummy's last heart. I can ruff my last heart in dummy and win the rest. I have used up my allotment of good luck for the next two years. I had to hope East had four clubs as well as the last missing trump. A 3-3 club break wouldn't have helped me.

It's sometimes right at matchpoints to play for down one in a 'normal' contract. My play could have resulted in down two but I judged that this contract wasn't normal: no other pairs would be in slam. Hence, our matchpoint score for -100 and -200 would have been the same.

25

In a Regional pairs event, I am blessed with an expert partner. Both sides are vulnerable and, as South, I hold:

♠ J 5 4 3
♡ K J 8 4
◇ A 9 5
♣ Q 3

West, the dealer, passes and my partner opens 1♣. The opponents pass throughout. I respond 1♡ and partner jumps to 3♠, a 'splinter' bid to show good heart support, spade shortness and slam interest.

Many experts view a splinter as a chance-giving action, appropriate even with a hand light in high-card values. It tells partner that slam is possible even if he has a minimum hand but no 'wasted' values opposite the shortness. In any case, my hand is worth a 4◇ cuebid and partner comes back with 4♠. He has a spade void or, more likely, the singleton ace.

A grand slam is possible. My hearts are decent. Partner has advertised a solid hand and is marked with club length; my queen will bolster his long suit. I bid 5NT. In some auctions, partner might interpret 5NT as 'pick a slam' but here he should treat it as a good old Grand Slam Force, asking him to bid seven with two of the top three honors in hearts, the agreed trump suit. He duly bids 7♡ and all pass. West leads the ♠10.

Dlr: West
Vul: Both

♠ A
♡ A Q 9 6
◇ K 8 4
♣ A K 10 8 2

♠ J 5 4 3
♡ K J 8 4
◇ A 9 5
♣ Q 3

West	North	East	South
pass	1♣	pass	1♡
pass	3♠	pass	4◇
pass	4♠	pass	5NT
pass	7♡	all pass	

That's roughly the dummy I expected. He has his bids. I can count ten tricks: a spade, four trumps, two diamonds and three clubs. If the clubs produce five tricks, my contract should be safe. Otherwise, I must ruff a club to establish the fifth club; plus, I will need two spade ruffs in dummy.

I think I can afford to test the trumps, so I take the AK. Both defenders follow politely. I cannot draw the missing trump. I ruff a spade in dummy, come to the ♣Q, ruff a spade and come back to the ◇A to draw the last trump. Then I take the ♣AK. West discards but I ruff a club and return to dummy with the ◇K to win the thirteenth trick with the good club. The full deal:

West	North / South	East
	♠ A ♡ A Q 9 6 ◇ K 8 4 ♣ A K 10 8 2	
♠ Q 10 9 8 ♡ 10 5 3 ◇ Q 10 3 2 ♣ 6 4	N W E S	♠ K 7 6 2 ♡ 7 2 ◇ J 7 6 ♣ J 9 7 5
	♠ J 5 4 3 ♡ K J 8 4 ◇ A 9 5 ♣ Q 3	

Our +2210 was worth 11 matchpoints out of 12. A couple of pairs mismanaged the play in 7♡ and some of the North-Souths who stopped in 6♡ made only six. (My impression is that slam bidding is a major weakness among pairs below the expert level.)

Bidding a close grand slam is questionable in a typical matchpoint field. Not every pair will bid seven and if thirteen tricks require astute play or a bit of luck, you can obtain a good result for being in six, making seven. That was the case here. If we had played in 6♡, making seven for +1460, we would have gotten 9 1/2. If 7♡ had failed, we would just have gotten a round zero. (A principle you have seen here before but well worth repeating.)

26

In a Regional Flighted Pairs, my partner is an exceedingly old-fashioned bidder. Our opponents are capable. Both sides are vulnerable and, as South, I hold:

♠ K Q J 10
♡ 6 2
◇ –
♣ J 10 9 7 5 4 3

West, the dealer, opens 1♡. My partner doubles and East raises to 2♡. My hand has a lot of potential; it might be right for me to jump straight to 4♠, making it harder for the opponents to find a five-level red-suit sacrifice or a make. But leaving my seven-card suit on the shelf looks extreme, so I try 3♣. I expect more bidding.

West bids 3◇, my partner passes and East goes back to 3♡. As I expected, I can now bid 3♠. It's true that I would usually bid spades first with four of them and that my partner may wonder whether I have four now. But after West passes, North raises me to 4♠. Everyone passes, West leads the ♡K and I await dummy with interest.

Dlr: West
Vul: Both

♠ A 7 6 5 2
♡ A 4
◇ A 8 6 2
♣ Q 2

♠ K Q J 10
♡ 6 2
◇ –
♣ J 10 9 7 5 4 3

West	North	East	South
1♡	dbl(!)	2♡	3♣
3◇	pass	3♡	3♠
pass	4♠	all pass	

North's double merits an exclamation mark. Few players would have doubled instead of overcalling 1♠. My partner still resides in the 'all-you-did-was-overcall' Dark Ages. Decades ago, a simple overcall tended to deny strength and good hands started with a double. In modern bidding, overcalls are wide-ranging. I once had a partner who informed me that she overcalled with as little — or as much — as she could get away with.

What of my chances in 4♠? I can see me making an overtrick if trumps are 2-2. Take the ♡A, discard my heart loser on the ◊A and start on the clubs. The defense can force me twice in the red suits but I can draw trumps, ending in my hand, and run the clubs. But if the trumps break 3-1, I will be in trouble. If they force me, I can still draw trumps but my club tricks will wither on the vine.

Remember to assess the contract when declaring at matchpoints. Consider whether you are in a 'normal' or 'abnormal' contract and tailor your play accordingly.

Maybe I should try to play safely for ten tricks. The contract looks worth ensuring. With West bidding both red suits, trumps are not likely to break evenly and East-West may have a paying save in 5♡. Not every North-South will get to 4♠ or be allowed to play there; a few may play in a partscore or in clubs.

Since I doubt that +620 will be a poor result, I take the ♡A and lead the ♣Q. East's king covers, and he cashes the ♡10 and shifts to the ◊4. I take dummy's ace and lead another club. East follows low and West takes the ace. I ruff the diamond return, draw trumps with the K-Q-J and claim. The full deal:

	♠ A 7 6 5 2 ♡ A 4 ◊ A 8 6 2 ♣ Q 2	
West ♠ 9 ♡ K Q J 7 5 ◊ K J 10 7 3 ♣ A 8	N W E S	**East** ♠ 8 4 3 ♡ 10 9 8 3 ◊ Q 9 5 4 ♣ K 6
	♠ K Q J 10 ♡ 6 2 ◊ – ♣ J 10 9 7 5 4 3	

As the cards lie, 4♠ fails if declarer quickly takes a heart discard on the ◊A. That happened at a couple of tables in my section.

At other tables, East-West played in 5♡ doubled. North-South could have been +800 in theory: ◊A opening lead, diamond ruff, ♠A, diamond ruff, ♡A. In practice, North led the ♠A. Even if South followed with the king to scream for a diamond switch and North obliged, the penalty was only +500. So, our result earned 70% of the matchpoints.

27

In a club duplicate, neither side is vulnerable and, as South, I hold:

♠ 7
♡ A 10 8 7 4 2
◇ A
♣ J 9 8 6 4

Ordinarily, it wouldn't occur to me to treat this 9-high-card-point hand as an opening bid. I would pass and hope to act later. But my partner for the day believes in the advantages of striking the first blow; he regularly reproaches me for my opening-bid standards, which he refers to as 'saurian'. So, I decide to live a little and experiment with a 1♡ opening. I do have two defensive tricks and the makings of some playing tricks. If I generate a disaster, it's only one board.

My partner responds 1♠, I rebid 2♣ and he jumps to 3♡. His jump-preference is invitational to game. If he had an opening bid with good heart support, he would bid 4♡ himself or maybe temporize with a 'fourth-suit' bid of 2◇.

We may be at a good matchpoint spot in a heart partial. For all I know, the deal may be passed out at some tables. If this were IMPs, I would bid 4♡ without a qualm. A pass would be defensible at matchpoints; nevertheless, I go ahead and try 4♡. I like my sixth heart and perhaps I can ruff some clubs in dummy.

All pass and West leads the ◇J. Dummy is about as advertised:

Dlr: South Vul: None	♠ Q 8 6 4 3 ♡ K 5 3 ♢ K Q 7 2 ♣ 7 ♠ 7 ♡ A 10 8 7 4 2 ♢ A ♣ J 9 8 6 4

West	North	East	South
			1♡(!)
pass	1♠	pass	2♣
pass	3♡	pass	4♡(!)
all pass			

This diamond opening lead seems to be helpful. I can take the ♢A, go to dummy with a trump and discard my spade loser on a high diamond; then, I can lead a club to set up a ruff. But I don't think that play will gain. If a defender wins the club and leads a second trump, he will deprive me of a club ruff and I'll just break even. Moreover, although I can also discard one club on dummy's second high diamond, my fifth club is likely to be set up anyway. I'll just be discarding a winner.

So, I decline to try for a fast discard: I lead a club on the second trick. West puts up the ten and shifts to the ♠J, winning. He then leads a trump. I take the king and East follows low. I discard two clubs on the ♢KQ, ruff a spade, ruff a club, ruff a spade and ruff my last club. East overruffs with the jack and leads a diamond, but I ruff low and claim when West can't overruff. Making four. The full deal:

♠ Q 8 6 4 3
♡ K 5 3
◇ K Q 7 2
♣ 7

West		East
♠ K J 10 2	N	♠ A 9 5
♡ 9	W E	♡ Q J 6
◇ J 10 9 8	S	◇ 6 5 4 3
♣ K 10 5 3		♣ A Q 2

♠ 7
♡ A 10 8 7 4 2
◇ A
♣ J 9 8 6 4

My decision to bid game turned out better than it deserved; West should have led a trump. He had strength everywhere: in my second suit, in dummy's spade suit and in diamonds. My most likely source of extra tricks was with ruffs. A trump lead would hold me to nine tricks.

At one table I heard about, South played 4♡ with the same ◇J lead. He won, led a trump to dummy, discarded a spade and a club on the top diamonds and led a club. East took the ace and led the ♡Q. Declarer could ruff one club in dummy but his last two clubs were losers and he also lost a trump to East for down one.

Our +420 was worth a tie for top; but if I play in 3♡ and take ten tricks for +170, we still score well above average. Minus 50 would have been a bottom. At matchpoints — even in a one-session duplicate, where you need lots of good results to win — the odds do not favor bidding speculative games. If making game requires luck or double-dummy play, you will get a good result if you take the maximum number of tricks. So it was in this deal.

On reflection, I wasn't sure my play was best. If trumps had split 2-2, I could have ensured ten tricks by taking the top trumps early. As it was, I risked a trump promotion at the end. Granted, a 2-2 break was only a 40% chance; but maybe West's failure to lead a trump should have led me to play differently.

28

In a Sectional Open Pairs, my partnership is having an atypically smooth game. On the next to last round, North, my partner, is the dealer with both sides vulnerable and, as South, I hold:

♠ K 7 5 4
♡ A K Q J 10 3
◇ 7
♣ J 5

North opens 1◇ and East overcalls 1♠. I bid 2♡, faintly wondering whether my hand might be worth a strong jump shift. West passes and North rebids 3♣. A 3♡ rebid by me would not be forcing and not especially encouraging. Even in a Two-over-One style, many pairs treat responder's minimum rebid of his own suit as not forcing, especially when the auction has been competitive. So, I jump to 4♡. Since slam is possible, I could have cuebid 2♠ and jumped to 4♡ next. If I had had the ♠A instead of the king, I would certainly have done that. All pass to my 4♡ and West leads the ♠6.

Dlr: North
Vul: Both

North:
♠ J 2
♡ 8
◇ A K 6 5 2
♣ A 9 6 3 2

South:
♠ K 7 5 4
♡ A K Q J 10 3
◇ 7
♣ J 5

West	North	East	South
	1◇	1♠	2♡
pass	3♣	pass	4♡
all pass			

East takes the ace and returns the ♠Q.

This is a matchpoints-versus-IMPs headache. I can see ten tricks: six trumps, two diamonds, a club and the ♠K. At IMPs, where my goal would be to make what I bid, I would play low on the second spade, preserving my king. If East led a third spade, I would play low again. If West had the ♡9, he could ruff in front of dummy for the defenders' third trick but I could take the rest.

Matchpoints is different. The goal is not to make game but to outscore the other North-South pairs. Here, my contract appears to be 'normal.' I expect every pair to be in the same spot. If I am +620 when everyone else is +650, I'll get a zero.

The ♠3 is missing and West may have it. If East had a six-card suit, he often would have made a weak jump overcall of 2♠. If I can win the second trick, I will have a chance for at least one overtrick. I can see ruffing a third spade with the ♡8 (if East has the nine) to get a dummy entry to set up the fifth diamond. So, I play the ♠K — and West ruffs and returns the ♡9.

Wonderful. I may have engineered myself into going down in a cold contract — the last thing I needed to do when we are having a good game. I mustn't give up. I run some trumps, hoping for a miracle. The cards when I lead my next-to-last trump are:

♠ –
♡ –
◇ A K 6 5
♣ A 9 6

♠ 7 5
♡ J 10
◇ 7
♣ J 5

West, who started with four trumps and has discarded a low club, lets go of the ♣10. He must be keeping four diamonds, lest I establish dummy's long diamond with a ruff. I discard a diamond from dummy and lead a club and when West plays the king, I let it hold. I win the diamond return and cash the ♣A and when the queen falls from West, I have the rest. The full deal:

♠ J 2
♡ 8
◇ A K 6 5 2
♣ A 9 6 3 2

West		East
♠ 6	N	♠ A Q 10 9 8 3
♡ 9 7 6 2	W E	♡ 5 4
◇ 9 8 4 3		◇ Q J 10
♣ K Q 10 8	S	♣ 7 4

♠ K 7 5 4
♡ A K Q J 10 3
◇ 7
♣ J 5

I survived a misplay. I should have given East credit for competent defense. If West wasn't going to ruff the second spade, East would not have returned a spade on the second trick. He might have led a trump or a club.

West could not beat 4♡ by leading the ♣K on the third trick. I could duck that, rectifying the count for a squeeze. If West led the ♣Q next (a diamond shift would be no better), I could win and run the trumps. At the end, West would have to save a high club and East a high spade, so neither defender could keep three diamonds.

29

In a Regional Flighted Pairs, we are up against an expert pair. As South, with both sides vulnerable, I hold:

♠ J 9 8 7 6 5
♡ 8
◇ 7 4
♣ K J 10 8

West, the dealer, passes and my partner opens 1♣. I scrape up a 1♠ response and he rebids 1NT. The opponents are silent.

I might consider a 2♣ preference since a club partial might offer a better chance for a plus score. As a practical matter, we wouldn't buy the contract in 2♣. Knowing that we have a trump fit and limited high-card strength, the expert opponents would surely balance and then I would have to bid 2♠ anyway. It must be better to bid 2♠ directly, making it harder for them to come in — for all I know, they may be cold for 4♡ — and at matchpoints, I want to play in the higher-scoring strain, even if it entails some risk.

When I rebid 2♠, everyone passes and West leads the ◇2.

Dlr: West
Vul: Both

♠ 10 3
♡ A K 7 4
◇ A J 5
♣ 5 4 3 2

♠ J 9 8 7 6 5
♡ 8
◇ 7 4
♣ K J 10 8

West	North	East	South
pass	1♣	pass	1♠
pass	1NT	pass	2♠
all pass			

That's a minimum my partner opened but he does have three defensive tricks and a ♢J supported by the ace. Nowadays, players routinely open with less.

I take the ♢A and hasten to cash the ♡AK to get rid of my diamond loser. Since I won't see dummy again, I lead a club next: six, jack, ace from West.

Things seem to be going well enough but West continues with the ♢K, forcing me to ruff. When I lead a trump on the sixth trick, West rises with the queen and leads a third diamond; I ruff again and lead another trump.

East wins with the king, cashes the ace and leads a fourth diamond, forcing out my last trump. I can only cash the ♣K and, when the queen doesn't fall, I lose the last two tricks to East, who has the ♣Q and a high heart. Down one, -100. The full deal:

	North	
	♠ 10 3 ♡ A K 7 4 ♢ A J 5 ♣ 5 4 3 2	
West ♠ Q 4 ♡ Q 10 9 6 3 ♢ K 10 6 2 ♣ A 9	N W E S	**East** ♠ A K 2 ♡ J 5 2 ♢ Q 9 8 3 ♣ Q 7 6
	♠ J 9 8 7 6 5 ♡ 8 ♢ 7 4 ♣ K J 10 8	

My partner and I exchange shrugs; the play seemed routine. But after the game, when a group of us adjourned to the bar to go over the deals, I learned that one declarer in our section had been +110 at the same 2♠ contract.

The opening lead was a diamond again, but the expert declarer foresaw the problems with keeping trump control. He took the ♢A and led a club to his jack!

West took the ace, cashed the ♢K and forced South to ruff a diamond; South then led a trump. When West took the queen, he couldn't profitably lead a fourth diamond, since dummy still had a trump. So, West shifted to a heart. Declarer won, finessed in clubs again and led a second trump. He wound up losing three trumps, a club and a diamond.

I had to admire South's play. I suppose my play could have worked and his could have come to grief but on reflection, I think his line was good. Actually, it was better than good.

30

I'm playing with an inexperienced but ebullient player in a club duplicate. With neither side vulnerable, I'm South, the dealer, and hold:

♠ K J 4
♡ K 7 3
◊ A
♣ A K Q J 7 4

If my long suit were a major, I might stretch to open 2♣. If my partner could provide a couple of queens, we might make game. As it is, I start with 1♣, hoping someone bids. My partner responds 1♡.

Now that partner has shown enough strength to respond, I must force to game — but I don't have a convenient force. A jump to 3♣ would be invitational, not forcing, and a jump to 3NT would be misdirected and might land us at a silly contract. I don't like it but I try 2♠. Jumping in a three-card suit, especially in spades, is asking for trouble. It might be safer to pretend I have diamonds and bid 2◊!

I'm hoping partner bids 2NT or 3♣ so that I can show my heart support next; but instead, he produces the bid I least want to hear: 3♠. Now I've brewed myself a pot of trouble. I can try 4♣ next or 4♡, but neither bid is likely to get me out of this fix. When I choose 4♣, partner persists with 4♠. Slam is still possible but I don't know whether it's safe to try. I decide to take my medicine in 4♠ and hope that, by some chance, it could be a winning contract.

West leads the ◊10 and partner puts down his dummy with an air of unconcern.

Dlr: South
Vul: None

♠ A Q 7 3
♡ Q 9 4 2
◇ J 7 3
♣ 5 2

♠ K J 4
♡ K 7 3
◇ A
♣ A K Q J 7 4

West	North	East	South
			1♣
pass	1♡	pass	2♠
pass	3♠	pass	4♣
pass	4♠	all pass	

Some players would have raised 2♠ directly to 4♠ with his hand to suggest good trumps but little else — perhaps as a 'Fast Arrival' action to deny slam interest. A practiced partnership would have discussed the nuances of raises to 3♠ and 4♠ but my partner and I had not. If I could have seen his hand, of course, I would have bid more.

I need to will myself to stay in the present and think about the play in 4♠. I can't do anything about pairs who reach 6♣, which is cold. One or two pairs may get to 6NT, which might make or fail, depending on whether the opening lead is a diamond. What I need is twelve tricks in spades for +480, beating any pairs who are playing at 3NT and are held to +460.

I take the ◇A and see that I need a heart trick. I don't have the dummy entries to take a diamond ruff in my hand and get back to draw trumps. But if I draw trumps and then lead a heart, the defense will be able to win and cash a couple of diamonds.

Suppose I try a heart to the queen at the second trick. If it wins, or if West grabs the ace and leads another diamond, I should be safe. But if the ♡Q loses to East, he will lead a diamond and I shall have to ruff. Then I'll have to rely on a 3-3 trump break, overtaking my jack in the dummy.

Thankfully, I see a solution. I lead the ♡K. If it wins, I will draw trumps and have twelve tricks with normal breaks in the black suits. East actually takes the ♡A and leads the ◇K but I can ruff, cash the ♠KJ and reach dummy with the ♡Q to draw trumps. The full deal:

	North	
	♠ A Q 7 3 ♡ Q 9 4 2 ◇ J 7 3 ♣ 5 2	
West ♠ 9 5 ♡ J 8 6 5 ◇ Q 10 9 4 ♣ 9 8 3	N W E S	**East** ♠ 10 8 6 2 ♡ A 10 ◇ K 8 6 5 2 ♣ 10 6
	♠ K J 4 ♡ K 7 3 ◇ A ♣ A K Q J 7 4	

I'm grateful that my partner appears not to notice that I only had three spades.

I made a dubious bid and survived. Our matchpoint result was actually above average. Only one pair got to slam and most of the pairs in 3NT got a diamond lead. The lesson is that when the auction doesn't go as you hope — maybe because you made a questionable bid — don't panic. Don't compound your error by making even more questionable bids.

31

In a local pairs game, my opponents are of average strength. Both sides are vulnerable and, as South, I hold:

♠ 5 2
♡ Q J 10 6 3 2
◊ A 7 3 2
♣ K

West deals and passes; two more passes follow. I suppose I might do best to pass the deal out. If I open and the opponents have a spade fit and half of the deck in high cards, we might get outbid and watch them score up +110 or +140. Still, I hate to cast my fate to a passout, especially in a one-session matchpoint event where we need good results to win. The opponents have shown no interest in bidding and for all I know, my partner has spades. So, I open 2♡. Everyone passes and I wait to see what I've gotten myself into.

West leads the ♠K.

Dlr: West
Vul: Both

North:
♠ 10 8 6
♡ A 9 8
◊ K Q 4
♣ 10 7 5 4

South:
♠ 5 2
♡ Q J 10 6 3 2
◊ A 7 3 2
♣ K

West	North	East	South
pass	pass	pass	2♡
all pass			

That dummy is a surprise. It looks like I might take nine or ten tricks; but even if I were to go down, -100 might be a good result against the spade partial the opponents surely could have made.

East signals with the queen on the first spade and West continues with a low spade. East wins with the nine and leads a third spade; when I ruff, West follows low.

The percentage play in trumps is to finesse but first, I'll find out who has the ♣A. I lead a diamond to dummy's king and return a club: nine, king, ace. West returns a club and I play low from dummy and ruff East's eight.

Now I know East has the ♡K — West never bid and has shown two aces and a king — so I pass up the finesse and lead a heart to the ace... and East's king falls!

I could take one more trump and then try the diamonds. I will win the rest if diamonds break 3-3 or if West, with the last missing trump, started with four diamonds. But that looks unlikely. West had three trumps and presumably four spades; if he had four diamonds, clubs would be divided 6-2, which is against the odds.

So, I choose to run all my trumps. As it happens, the full deal is:

	North	
	♠ 10 8 6 ♡ A 9 8 ♢ K Q 4 ♣ 10 7 5 4	
West ♠ A K 7 3 ♡ 7 5 4 ♢ 9 6 ♣ A 6 3 2	N W E S	**East** ♠ Q J 9 4 ♡ K ♢ J 10 8 5 ♣ Q J 9 8
	♠ 5 2 ♡ Q J 10 6 3 2 ♢ A 7 3 2 ♣ K	

When I lead my last trump, East is squeezed. He has room for three cards and must keep the ♣Q, since dummy still has the ten. So, he throws a diamond and my fourth diamond wins the thirteenth trick.

Making four. I'm glad I judged not to pass the deal out. West couldn't have done better by leading a second diamond when he took the ♣A. There are squeeze possibilities and I can always take ten tricks.

Our +170 was worth most of the matchpoints, but the result was mostly due to East-West's timidity in the auction. Most East-Wests got in somehow. Many Wests opened the bidding. At tables where South was left to open 2♡ in fourth position, some Wests risked a double or, if West and North passed, some Easts balanced with a double — an aggressive action that the matchpoint conditions supported. When East-West bought the deal in a spade partial, declarer took at least nine tricks.

32

In a Sectional Swiss Teams, both sides are vulnerable and, as South, I hold:

♠ 7 3
♡ A K Q J 10 9
◇ A 2
♣ K 9 6

West, the dealer, opens 2◇, weak. That use of 2◇ seems to be going the way of the dinosaurs; pairs agree to treat the bid in other ways. I have a friend who is sold on the Roman 2◇ opening, which shows a minimum three-suited hand. That convention is not my favorite and in my book, *Keys to Winning Bridge*, I included a critique of it. I wrote that it doesn't come up often enough to make it worthwhile, that opening at the two-level with minimum values and no assurance of a fit is risky and that the auction may beg for a killer trump opening lead. My friend told me he read my critique — and gave up reading. Like many players, he cherishes his pet conventions.

Two passes follow and I must choose an action. I suppose I could start with a double, intending to bid hearts next, or I could jump directly to 3♡ — a strong-ish action. Instead, I judge to play my partner for a bit of strength and I take the pressure off: I bid 4♡ and everyone passes.

West leads the ◇Q and dummy is no better than I deserve.

Dlr: West
Vul: Both

♠ Q 9 4
♡ 8 5 4
◇ K 8 6 5
♣ Q 8 2

♠ 7 3
♡ A K Q J 10 9
◇ A 2
♣ K 9 6

West	North	East	South
2◇	pass	pass	4♡
all pass			

Only nine tricks! I could have preferred a more disciplined route and let North use his judgment. Still, the contract isn't hopeless. I take the ♢A and draw trumps, finding West with a singleton. He discards two diamonds. Now, I could attack the clubs, hoping for a friendly lie; but if West has Ax or doubleton J10, he would have 4-1-6-2-shape and not many Wests would open 2♢ with four cards in spades. Anyway, I'm in no hurry. On the fifth trick, I lead a spade to dummy's nine.

East wins with the jack, cashes the king and leads the ace. I ruff and West discards a club. Now I know his pattern was 2-1-6-4 and I expect that he had the ♣A for his bid. I'm assuming the position is:

West	North	East
	♠ —	
	♡ —	
	♢ K 8 6	
	♣ Q 8 2	
♠ —	N	♠ 6 5
♡ —	W E	♡ —
♢ J 10 9	S	♢ —
♣ A J 4		♣ 10 7 5
	♠ —	
	♡ 10 9	
	♢ 2	
	♣ K 9 6	

When I cash another trump, West is in difficulty. If he throws another club, I throw a diamond from dummy, lead a club to the queen and duck on the way back. West actually discards a diamond, so I pitch a club from dummy, lead to the ♢K, ruff a diamond to set up dummy's last diamond and lead a club. Making four. The full deal:

	North	
	♠ Q 9 4 ♡ 8 5 4 ♢ K 8 6 5 ♣ Q 8 2	
West ♠ 10 8 ♡ 2 ♢ Q J 10 9 7 3 ♣ A J 4 3	N W E S	**East** ♠ A K J 6 5 2 ♡ 7 6 3 ♢ 4 ♣ 10 7 5
	♠ 7 3 ♡ A K Q J 10 9 ♢ A 2 ♣ K 9 6	

East couldn't afford to shift to a club when he was in; that would have cost the defense a club trick.

At the other table, the auction started the same way but South reopened with 3NT, an action I might have considered. It turned out to be a winning call. Everyone passed and West led the ♢Q. Declarer took the ace and immediately led a club. My teammate in West, who couldn't see all four hands and wasn't sure what declarer was up to, played low; when the queen won in dummy, South claimed nine tricks. So, we gained a solitary IMP.

33

In a local Knockout Teams semifinal, our opponents are competent. We had a slight lead at halftime. On the first deal after the break, neither side is vulnerable and as South, the dealer, I pick up:

♠ Q J 7 4 3
♡ 6 4 2
◇ A J 10
♣ A 4

I open 1♠. I would rather have a high-card point or two more, or at least some spade intermediates, but passing this decent 12-point hand would be a deep position. Most players would open with less.

The opponents stay out and my partner jumps to 4♣, a splinter response. He has a big spade fit, club shortness (usually a singleton, though some players would not splinter with a singleton ace) and at least mild slam interest.

I must judge whether to move toward slam. My ♣A is an ideal card — if my clubs were KQ4, the honors would be 'wasted' — and my diamond holding is encouraging as well. Partner's high-card strength may well include a diamond honor. Still, my hand is a minimum in terms of high cards, my trumps are only fair and I'm looking at three heart losers. So, I sign off in 4♠ and everyone passes. West leads the ♣Q.

Dlr: South
Vul: None

North:
♠ A K 8 6 2
♡ A Q 5 3
◇ 7 4 3
♣ 6

South:
♠ Q J 7 4 3
♡ 6 4 2
◇ A J 10
♣ A 4

West	North	East	South
			1♠
pass	4♣	pass	4♠
all pass			

I'm glad we stopped in 4♠; I would be nervous playing in a higher contract. Still, ten tricks look easy enough. I have nine — five trumps in my hand, three side-suit aces and a club ruff in dummy — and plenty of chances for one more. Surely one of them will come to pass.

Contracts that look easy require extra care. What can go wrong? Suppose that the hearts are lying badly and both diamond honors are offside as well. Eventually, I come up with a line of play that will guarantee the contract. I may be pitching an IMP but I will make the investment. I take the ♣A, ruff my low club, cash the ♠Q and the ♡A, draw trumps and lead a heart from my hand. West follows with the ten and I play low from dummy.

The full deal:

	North	
	♠ A K 8 6 2 ♡ A Q 5 3 ◇ 7 4 3 ♣ 6	
West ♠ 10 9 5 ♡ 10 8 ◇ K Q 6 ♣ Q J 10 5 3	N / W E / S	**East** ♠ — ♡ K J 9 7 ◇ 9 8 5 2 ♣ K 9 8 7 2
	♠ Q J 7 4 3 ♡ 6 4 2 ◇ A J 10 ♣ A 4	

The defenders cannot untangle themselves. If East lets the ten win, West has to lead a helpful diamond for me or concede a ruff-and-sluff. (If West had a heart left and led it, I would play dummy's queen and would be sure of a second heart trick and a diamond discard.)

As it is, East overtakes with the ♡J and leads a diamond I play the ten and when West wins, he is endplayed again. My line ensured the contract no matter how the red suits lay.

At the other table, South surprisingly declined to open the bidding. North opened 1♠ and played in 4♠ and East inconvenienced declarer by leading a diamond. The contract could (and perhaps should) have been made but wasn't; we gained 10 IMPs.

The idea behind splinter bids (and calls such as mini-splinters) is to let you judge whether you have useful or wasted values opposite the shortness. Two hands that fit together well may produce slam or game despite a high-card minimum.

In my experience, players tend to use splinter bids too readily, looking for miracle fits. In the deal above, North's hand was (in my opinion) a dead minimum for his 4♣ response. Maybe he thought he had no options. He could have responded 2NT as a conventional forcing raise but that response would suggest balanced distribution.

34

When I attended NABCs, I spent as much time watching as playing. One of the most careful and deliberate players I ever kibitzed was the late Norman Kay, a wonderful technician as well as one of the game's great gentlemen. One of my regrets is that I never got to have a game with him.

The story goes that Kay became declarer in a slam at a Team Trials. After the opening lead, he withdrew into the grandfather of all huddles. He made the slam but the opponents complained to the director about slow play.

"Look," they said, "it was a routine contract. The only possible problem was a 5-0 trump break."

The director approached Kay. "Norman," he asked, "why did you take so long on that slam?"

"I was wondering what I would do if trumps broke 5-0," Kay replied sheepishly.

In a local Swiss Teams, both sides are vulnerable and, as South, I hold:

♠ A Q 10 9 5
♡ A Q 7 6 2
◇ Q 5 3
♣ –

My partner deals and opens 1◇, I respond 1♠ and West jumps to 3♣, preemptive. After two passes, I try 3♡. If the overcall had been 2♣, there would be a case for my partner to treat a 2♡ bid by me as competitive and not forcing. But a bid of a new suit by responder (if he is not a passed hand) is generally regarded as forcing. I certainly don't think my partner will pass when I've come back in at the three-level.

Instead, North jumps to 4♠. He must have a sound hand and decent three-card spade support. If he has little 'wasted' strength in clubs opposite my void, we can probably make a slam. Give him:

♠ K J 4 ♡ K 5 ◇ A J 10 4 2 ♣ J 6 5

and I would have play for thirteen tricks.

I think this is my gamble to take. North probably did his all when he jumped to 4♠. So, I bid 6♠. If I go down, it won't be for the first time.

West leads the ♣A.

Dlr: North
Vul: Both

♠ K 3 2
♡ 8 4
◇ A K J 9 7
♣ K 7 6

♠ A Q 10 9 5
♡ A Q 7 6 2
◇ Q 5 3
♣ —

West	North	East	South
	1◇	pass	1♠
3♣	pass	pass	3♡
pass	4♠	pass	6♠
all pass			

That's about as weak a dummy as I could have expected, with the ♣K wasted; but I still have a chance, especially with this opening lead, which makes a winner out of dummy's ♣K. I can ruff, pick up the trumps even if they break 4-1 (presumably, only East can have four), run the diamonds and take the ♣K. If trumps break 3-2, I can afford to finesse in hearts at the end to try for an overtrick.

But the possibility of trouble flits through my mind. What if trumps break 5-0? After West's vulnerable preempt, the chance of bad breaks goes way up. I think it might pay to pitch a heart on the first trick, preserving my trump length. If I ruff and find East with five trumps, I won't be able to run the diamonds.

When his ♣A wins, West leads the ♣Q. That's fine; a diamond shift would have made me nervous. I discard another heart on the ♣K and cash the ♠K just in case... and West throws a club! I lead a trump to my ten, return a diamond to dummy, lead a trump to my nine and take the ♠AQ. Then I can run the diamonds and take the ♡A for twelve tricks. The full deal:

	North	
	♠ K 3 2 ♡ 8 4 ♢ A K J 9 7 ♣ K 7 6	
West ♠ — ♡ K 5 3 ♢ 10 8 6 ♣ A Q J 10 8 5 4	N W E S	**East** ♠ J 8 7 6 4 ♡ J 10 9 ♢ 4 2 ♣ 9 3 2
	♠ A Q 10 9 5 ♡ A Q 7 6 2 ♢ Q 5 3 ♣ —	

If declarer ruffs the opening lead, the slam fails. Thanks for the help, Norman.

35

In a Sectional Swiss Teams, my team has been unlucky and lost its opening match. (Our opponents played a lot better than we did and nothing is unluckier than being outplayed.) We can't afford more such adversity. On the first deal of the second match, neither side is vulnerable and, as South, I hold:

♠ A Q 7 5 2
♡ K 8 4
◇ A Q J 4
♣ 8

West, the dealer, opens 1♣, and two passes follow. In the 'balancing' position, I'm too heavy for 1♠; I would choose that call with a much weaker hand. Instead, I start with a double. If my partner responds, say, 1♡, I will continue with 1♠ to suggest a sound hand, not a balancing type of hand with shaded values. If he passes my double for penalty, that will be fine with me.

West rebids 1♡, my partner passes and East gives preference with 2♣. I don't like this; my ♡K may now be a worthless card and if my partner has club values and no spade tolerance, we may go plus only if I pass and defend. Still, I hate to sell out at the two-level when the opponents appear to have a fit of sorts, so I take a chance and try 2♠.

Everyone passes, not totally to my liking, and West leads the ♠10.

Dlr: West
Vul: None

♠ K J
♡ 7 5 3 2
◇ 8 5 2
♣ 10 9 3 2

♠ A Q 7 5 2
♡ K 8 4
◇ A Q J 4
♣ 8

West	North	East	South
1♣	pass	pass	dbl
1♡	pass	2♣	2♠
all pass			

I suppose that's a better dummy than I deserve. Assuming a decent trump break, I can see seven tricks. To make 2♠, I'll need two extra diamonds. I take the ♠KJ — the opponents follow — and lead a diamond. Finessing can't be right. I can place East with a high club — no doubt the king — since West would surely have led a high club if he held the AK or KQ. I take the ♢A and then the ♠AQ, finding that West had a doubleton. He discards two low clubs.

I wonder whether I should lead the ♢Q next. East didn't respond to West's opening bid and has at most 5 high-card points (and these days, many players are willing to respond with fewer). So I can place West with 16 or so points, but then with balanced distribution, he would have opened 1NT. I think I can give West 2-4-2-5 shape.

I back my convictions and lead the ♢4. Fortunately, the full deal is:

	North	
	♠ K J ♡ 7 5 3 2 ♢ 8 5 2 ♣ 10 9 3 2	
West ♠ 10 9 ♡ A Q J 6 ♢ K 6 ♣ A Q J 6 4	N / W E / S	**East** ♠ 8 6 4 3 ♡ 10 9 ♢ 10 9 7 3 ♣ K 7 5
	♠ A Q 7 5 2 ♡ K 8 4 ♢ A Q J 4 ♣ 8	

When West's ♢K pops up, I have my eight tricks.

In the replay, my teammate as West opened a slightly offshape 1NT. Knowing him as I do, I fear that he might have made the same call with:

♠ 10 9 3 ♡ A Q J 6 ♢ K ♣ A Q J 6 4

— something that would give me indigestion. After two passes, South had an awkward problem and passed. No guarantee went with bidding 2♠ (though he might have made that contract: only the opening lead of a low or middle club can beat it).

Against 1NT, North led a heart. Declarer raced off nine tricks for +150, so we gained 6 IMPs.

36

In a local Swiss Teams, my partner is a promising intermediate player. The opponents are reasonably capable. Both sides are vulnerable and, as North, I pick up:

♠ K 6 4
♡ 9 6 2
◇ A 7 5 3
♣ A Q 8

West, the dealer, opens 1♡. I have an opening hand but doubling wouldn't occur to me. My hand is full of losers — three in hearts just for starters — and would be a terrible dummy to put down if I doubled and compelled my partner to bid something. If I held a bit more strength —

♠A J 6 4 ♡9 6 2 ◇A 7 5 ♣A Q 8

— with no heart honors that might prove useful for defense, I would double. With:

♠A 8 6 4 ♡Q 6 2 ◇A 7 5 ♣K J 8

I would pass.

East passes and my partner balances with 1♠. His hand can be quite weak — he may have stretched to keep the opponents from buying the deal cheaply — but I still have enough to try for game. After West passes, I cuebid 2♡ and my partner bids 2♠.

Maybe I should let him out below game but we're vulnerable and a club finesse, if we need it, should work. Moreover, partner should be aided in the play because he will know that most or all of the missing points reside with West. So, I raise to 4♠.

All pass and West leads the ◇10.

Dlr: West
Vul: Both

♠ K 6 4
♡ 9 6 2
♢ A 7 5 3
♣ A Q 8

♠ A J 8 7 3
♡ J 5
♢ K 6 2
♣ J 10 9

West	North	East	South
1♡	pass	pass	1♠
pass	2♡	pass	2♠
pass	4♠	all pass	

"If you don't make it," I tell my partner, "it's my fault."

He wins with the ♢K, leads a trump to the king and returns a trump. East follows with the deuce and ten; my partner consults the ceiling and... finesses with the jack. West produces the queen and, though the club finesse wins later, partner loses two hearts and a diamond for down one. The full deal:

North:
♠ K 6 4
♡ 9 6 2
♢ A 7 5 3
♣ A Q 8

West:
♠ Q 5
♡ A Q 10 7 3
♢ Q 10 9 4
♣ K 5

East:
♠ 10 9 2
♡ K 8 4
♢ J 8
♣ 7 6 4 3 2

South:
♠ A J 8 7 3
♡ J 5
♢ K 6 2
♣ J 10 9

At the other table, North doubled the 1♡ opening and South jumped to 2♠, inviting game. North passed, of course. They were +140, and we lost 6 IMPs instead of gaining 10.

My partner told me he wasn't sure how to play the trumps. West was likely to have the queen but could have had an opening bid without it; plus, with an eight-card holding, a finesse was the percentage play.

My partner missed an inference. East had not responded to the opening bid and therefore had at most 5 high-card points. If West's hearts had been AKxxx or KQ10xx, his opening lead would have been a high heart, so East was almost sure to have the king. The opening lead also marked East with the ♢J, so he couldn't have the ♠Q. Declarer should have played to drop the queen. (A similar inference to the one on the previous deal.)

37

Deals in which declarer must count out the distribution of the concealed hands — say, to place a missing queen — occur occasionally. But counting declarer's distribution (and his high-card points and potential winners) is essential to the defense in every deal. To play tight defense without counting is impossible.

In a local Swiss Teams, neither side is vulnerable. I am East and my partner is a club player who tends to be aggressive. My hand is:

♠ Q 9 6 4 2
♡ K 10 7 3
◇ 10 9
♣ A 6

South, the dealer, opens 1◇, my partner doubles and North raises to 2◇. My hand is quite promising; I may have play for game even opposite one of my partner's skinny doubles. I could cuebid 3◇ to get both majors into the picture, but to avoid inflaming his passions, I jump to 3♠ — maybe a slight underbid.

South competes with 4◇ and West bids 4♠. Inviting game with him is like waving a red flag under a bull's nose. I expect all pass but, after two passes, South persists with 5◇. After two more passes, I have to use my judgment.

I could pass. I have no assurance that we could have made 4♠, and South may have bid 5◇ to make, not as a sacrifice. But I suppose I must treat partner's pass as forcing, judging that the opponents have saved. Maybe we can take three tricks in defense. After all, I have some high-card values and partner doubled. It is possible we need to collect +300 because East-West at the other table will get +170 in a spade partial.

My double is passed out and my partner leads the ♠7.

Dlr: South Vul: None	♠ 10 5 ♡ Q 8 ♢ K 7 4 3 ♣ Q 7 4 3 2	
	N W E S	♠ Q 9 6 4 2 ♡ K 10 7 3 ♢ 10 9 ♣ A 6

West	**North**	**East**	**South**
			1♢
dbl	2♢	3♠	4♢
4♠	pass	pass	5♢
pass	pass	dbl	all pass

I play the queen and South takes the ace and leads the ♣5. My partner huddles and plays the nine; dummy ducks. When partner tries to cash the ♠K, declarer ruffs and takes the ♢KA. West follows with the queen, then discards a spade. Next comes the ♣8: ten, low... and I take the ace. That leaves me on lead in this uneasy position:

	♠ — ♡ Q 8 ♢ 7 4 ♣ Q 7 4	
	N W E S	♠ 9 6 4 ♡ K 10 7 3 ♢ — ♣ —

Declarer is marked with 1-4-6-2 distribution. He wouldn't play the clubs in that way — without drawing trumps — if he had K85 or J85. Despite my partner's aggressive bidding, I expect South to have the ♡A. If he doesn't, he opened with a nine-count and then bid strongly. So a heart return will surely be fatal but a spade will concede a ruff-and-sluff.

Let me count declarer's tricks. If I return a spade and he ruffs in dummy, he will still have a heart to lose, assuming that my partner holds the jack. If, instead, declarer ruffs in his hand and discards a heart from dummy, he can take six trumps in his hand, the ♠A, ♡A and two heart ruffs in dummy… but he will still be a trick short.

So I lead a third spade; the full deal is:

	North	
	♠ 10 5 ♡ Q 8 ◇ K 7 4 3 ♣ Q 7 4 3 2	
West ♠ K J 8 7 3 ♡ J 6 5 ◇ Q ♣ K J 10 9	N / W E / S	**East** ♠ Q 9 6 4 2 ♡ K 10 7 3 ◇ 10 9 ♣ A 6
	♠ A ♡ A 9 4 2 ◇ A J 8 6 5 2 ♣ 8 5	

South has to go down one and we have huffed and puffed our way to +100. West could have made things easier if he had shifted to a heart on the third trick; but he didn't know I had the ♡10. (That was some 4♠ bid my partner found!)

At the other table, my teammate in South opened 1◇ but West overcalled 1♠. North raised to 2◇ and East bid up to 4♠. South had a tough call. He might have bid 5◇ since a North hand such as:

♠ 10 5 ♡ 5 3 ◇ K 7 4 3 ♣ A 7 4 3 2

would have been enough to make it. But North could have held:

♠ 10 5 ♡ K 5 3 ◇ K 7 4 3 ♣ J 7 6 4

and then both 5◇ and 4♠ might fail. South had promising defense — three aces — so he judged to defend. Unfortunately, North led a diamond instead of the ♡Q and when South took the ace, he led a second diamond. The defenders' potential heart ruff vanished and, with the hearts sitting well for declarer, 4♠ was unbeatable.

So East-West were +420 and we lost 8 IMPs. Such are the fortunes of war.

38

In a local Swiss Teams, my partner is an aspiring intermediate player. Our opponents are more experienced. Neither side is vulnerable and, as West, I hold:

♠ 8 4
♡ J 10 9 6 3
◇ K J 5 2
♣ A 10

South, the dealer, opens 1♣. I refrain from overcalling; I know plenty of successful players who would act with a weaker hand but my style is based on sound initial actions. North responds 1♠, South rebids 1NT and North raises to 3NT. I lead the ♡J.

Dlr: South
Vul: None

North:
♠ K Q J 9 3
♡ K 5
◇ 10 8 4
♣ K 6 3

West:
♠ 8 4
♡ J 10 9 6 3
◇ K J 5 2
♣ A 10

West	North	East	South
			1♣
pass	1♠	pass	1NT
pass	3NT	all pass	

Declarer puts up dummy's king, winning as my partner follows with the deuce. South plays the four. Next, dummy leads the ♣3: five, queen... and I take my ace.

I have options. I could plug away at the hearts, though my partner should have unblocked the queen if he had it. I could return the ♣10 since East might have started with J-9-x-x. I could risk a diamond shift.

In such situations, a defender must try to reconstruct declarer's hand from the bidding and play. I know he had at most 15 high-card points — their 1NT range is 16 to 18 — and presumably balanced distribution. It's possible he might have bid that way with 1-4-4-4 shape, but I can't defend on an unlikely assumption.

South has shown the ♡A and ♣Q. He surely has the ♠A. If his spades were 10x or xxx, his first move would have been to set up dummy's suit. Nor would he have won the first heart with the king which, from his point of view, might be dummy's only entry. (He wouldn't have known that I was holding the ♣A.)

South may have the ♡Q or ♣J but, even if he lacks both of those honors, he can't have the ◇AQ, giving him 16 high-card points. In fact, if South has the ◇A, we are not beating this. He has five spade tricks, three hearts, a club and a diamond. So, on the third trick, I shift to the ◇2. The full deal is:

	North	
	♠ K Q J 9 3 ♡ K 5 ◇ 10 8 4 ♣ K 6 3	
♠ 8 4 ♡ J 10 9 6 3 ◇ K J 5 2 ♣ A 10	N W E S	♠ 10 6 5 2 ♡ 8 2 ◇ A 7 3 ♣ 9 8 5 2
	♠ A 7 ♡ A Q 7 4 ◇ Q 9 6 ♣ Q J 7 4	

Unfortunately, my shift bore no fruit. My partner took the ◇A and started to think. If your partners are like some of mine, that portends disaster. Sure enough, East returned the ♡8 and South happily cashed ten tricks for +430.

At the other table, our teammates got to 4♠ by North via an auction I wasn't privileged to hear about. Luckily, East didn't get his fingers on the ◇A; he led a heart. Declarer won with the king, drew trumps and cashed two more top hearts for a diamond discard. He lost two diamonds and a club for +420: a push.

My partner's heart return was wrong. At the vulnerability, I would have acted with ♡AJ10xxx. Moreover, my ◇2 — a low diamond — canceled my interest in hearts and asked for a diamond return. If I had wanted East to win and go back to hearts, I would have led a high diamond.

As to my placing South with the ♠A... When a capable declarer fails to attack a long, strong suit in dummy, a sound inference is available. Either he has none of that suit — impossible in this deal — or the suit is already established.

39

I was having my annual physical recently and it occurred to me to ask my doctor how he determined whether an elderly patient might be in need of assisted care.

"I put some water in a tub," the doc replied, "give the patient a spoon, a cup and a bucket and ask him to empty the tub."

"And anyone who doesn't use the bucket is on the brink?" I asked.

"Anyone who doesn't pull the plug may be."

If a lack of clear thinking at the table is a problem for you, defend this deal. In the first match after the dinner break in a Sectional Swiss Teams, both sides are vulnerable and, as West, I hold:

♠ 8 6
♡ 10 9 6 4 2
◇ A J 6 2
♣ A 2

South, the dealer, opens 1♣ and I pass. Even at favorable vulnerability, overcalling 1♡ wouldn't occur to me, though it might to some players a lot younger than I. North responds 1♠, South rebids 1NT, North raises to 2NT and South goes on to 3NT.

We ask and are told that the opponents' range to open 1NT is 16 to 18 points. At matchpoints, most pairs use a 15-to-17 range and open many 12-point hands; therefore, if a 1NT rebid can show from 12 to 15 points, that 4-point range is unwieldy. At IMPs, where bidding good games and avoiding disasters are the goals, it is sensible to play a slightly higher range: maybe a 'good' 15 to 18. So, South could have as many as 15 points and, since he accepted a game invitation, will have no fewer than 14.

I lead the ♡4.

Dlr: South
Vul: Both

North:
♠ A Q J 7 5
♡ Q 7
♢ 9 7 5
♣ Q 6 5

West:
♠ 8 6
♡ 10 9 6 4 2
♢ A J 6 2
♣ A 2

West	North	East	South
			1♣
pass	1♠	pass	1NT
pass	2NT	pass	3NT
all pass			

Declarer puts up dummy's queen, winning as my partner plays the three. Dummy then leads a club: jack, king... and I take the ace. Pairs have varying agreements about a defender's second-hand play from a sequential holding. To me, my partner's ♣J suggests a sequence headed by the jack.

I have options. I can continue hearts, return a club to set up partner's intermediates in that suit or try a diamond switch. It's easier to defend well if you know what declarer has, so I try to figure it out. I know he had the ♡AK and the ♣K. Moreover, I am sure he has the ♠K. If his spade holding were, say, 103, he would have attacked the spades as his first move. He wouldn't have played clubs, which might have set up tricks for us. Nor would declarer have won the first heart with the queen, expending what might have been dummy's only entry to the long spades.

So declarer can't have the ♢K: that would give him 16 points — too many for his bidding. On the third trick, I shift to the ♢2. My partner produces the king and huddles. I'm afraid that he might shift back to hearts but my ♢2 did show interest in diamonds. If I had wanted partner to win and return a heart, I would have led the highest diamond I could find. Eventually, partner returns a diamond and the full deal is:

	North	
	♠ A Q J 7 5 ♡ Q 7 ♢ 9 7 5 ♣ Q 6 5	
West ♠ 8 6 ♡ 10 9 6 4 2 ♢ A J 6 2 ♣ A 2	N / W E / S	**East** ♠ 9 4 3 ♡ J 8 3 ♢ K 4 3 ♣ J 10 9 8
	♠ K 10 2 ♡ A K 5 ♢ Q 10 8 ♣ K 7 4 3	

We take four diamonds and a club for down one.

At the other table, my teammate in South opened 1NT, perhaps appreciating his two tens. North transferred to spades and bid 3NT, offering a choice of games. Personally, I might have taken my chances in 3NT; but my teammate removed to 4♠.

West led the ♡4 and declarer won with the queen. Double-dummy, he could have succeeded by drawing trumps, cashing two more top hearts to discard a diamond from dummy and playing West for Ax in clubs. Instead, he took the ♠10 and ♠Q and next let the ♢9 ride, hoping to win his tenth trick with the ♢Q. He lost three diamonds and the ♣A for down one. Just a push, in the end.

You should find this point similar to the one on the previous deal.

40

In a session of bridge, you will have good results and bad. You will make good plays and, no matter who you are, you will make errors. The goddess of chance will see that some of your results are beyond your control.

Winning players remain thoroughly impassive. They stay in the present. They know that an emotional response to any result — or even to the play of a single trick — can adversely affect their focus on the next trick or deal.

This is a deal from a local Swiss Teams in which my partner slipped. I was grateful not to be sitting in his seat. Although I've been around long enough to know better, I might have made the same error. Try it as a problem.

Dlr: South
Vul: None

North:
♠ J 6 4 2
♡ Q 9 3
♢ A 7 6
♣ Q 10 5

West:
♠ A 9 7 3
♡ 8 7 5
♢ Q 9 2
♣ A K 7

West	North	East	South
			1NT[1]
pass	2♣	pass	2♢
pass	2NT	all pass	

1. 15 to 17.

Say you lead the ♠3: deuce, ten, king. Declarer leads a diamond to dummy's ace and returns a diamond to his jack. East follows with the five and ten. Plan your defense.

The full deal was:

	♠ J 6 4 2 ♡ Q 9 3 ◇ A 7 6 ♣ Q 10 5	
♠ A 9 7 3 ♡ 8 7 5 ◇ Q 9 2 ♣ A K 7	N W E S	♠ Q 10 5 ♡ J 10 4 2 ◇ 10 5 ♣ 9 8 4 2
	♠ K 8 ♡ A K 6 ◇ K J 8 4 3 ♣ J 6 3	

At the other table, where our teammates were North-South, South opened 1NT, showing 14 to 16 points, a range that somehow tends to prove awkward. North wasn't tempted to try for game. West led the ♣K and East, with no great desire for a shift, encouraged with the nine. West continued with the ♣A and a third club. Declarer won, cashed the ◇A and lost a diamond finesse to West. West exited with his last diamond. Declarer took his eight tricks for +120.

At our table, South's 1NT promised 15 to 17 points and North-South reached 2NT on the auction shown. My partner, West, led the ♠3: deuce, ten, king. Declarer went to the ◇A and finessed with the jack. West won and, after a modest pause for thought, led the ♠9: low from dummy, five from me, eight!

My partner must have been inwardly exultant. He promptly led a third spade to my queen. But then I had to guess what to return. Maybe I should have found the club return that would have beaten 2NT. It was the kind of situation that keeps players awake at night, wondering whether there was any way they could have known. As it was, I led a heart and declarer claimed eight tricks for +120. Instead of gaining 6 IMPs, we pushed the board.

My partner fell victim to what I call the 'Euphoria Effect' (and Euphoria is not one of the Nine Muses of Greek myth). He was so delighted at having pinned declarer's ♠8 that he forgot the deal wasn't over. At the fourth trick, West needed to cash his ♣K. Then, when I was in with the ♠Q, I would know what to do next.

Don't let euphoria ruin the effect of a good play you made. Maintain your focus.

41

This is a deal in which I had a fixation. That is a fault that can victimize experienced players. They are so focused on one aspect of a deal that they overlook a vital secondary point. (As I know well, the problem can afflict writers also.)

In a Sectional Swiss Teams, neither side is vulnerable and I am sitting East with:

♠ K 9 5 2
♡ 6 5
◇ A K 7
♣ 7 6 5 2

North, to my right, opens 1♣ and our side does not enter the auction. South responds 1♡, North rebids 1♠ and South jumps to 4♡, passed out. My partner leads the ◇5, the only unbid suit, and I see:

Dlr: North
Vul: None

North:
♠ A 7 4 3
♡ 9 4
◇ J 6 4
♣ A K J 10

East:
♠ K 9 5 2
♡ 6 5
◇ A K 7
♣ 7 6 5 2

West	North	East	South
	1♣	pass	1♡
pass	1♠	pass	4♡
all pass			

Dummy plays low, my ◇K wins and South follows with the three. How should I continue?

I don't like our prospects of beating this contract. South surely has six or seven good hearts and if his suit is solid, he will take the rest after we cash whatever diamond tricks we have coming. If he needs a club finesse, it will win. Assuming that my partner has a trick in trumps to give us a chance, how can we take three more tricks?

I suspect we will need a spade trick — and quickly, before declarer draws trumps and uses the clubs to get a discard. If my partner has the ♠Q, I can lead a spade safely; even if declarer has the queen, he will have a guess if he has Q10. So on the second trick, I shift smoothly to the ♠2.

Declarer thinks that over and plays the ten: jack, ace. South then lets the ♡9 ride. West produces the queen and leads a spade; I take the king. When the queen falls from South, I cash my ◇A for down one. The full deal:

	♠ A 7 4 3 ♡ 9 4 ◇ J 6 4 ♣ A K J 10	
♠ J 8 6 ♡ Q 7 3 ◇ Q 10 8 5 2 ♣ 9 8	N W E S	♠ K 9 5 2 ♡ 6 5 ◇ A K 7 ♣ 7 6 5 2
	♠ Q 10 ♡ A K J 10 8 2 ◇ 9 3 ♣ Q 4 3	

A first-round finesse was declarer's correct percentage play in trumps, gaining whenever East had Qxxx. Declarer might instead have taken the AK, then tried to get a discard on dummy's clubs. That approach would have failed too.

I was pleased but my partner glowered at me and South looked like he was upset with me as well.

"I assumed the man knew what he was doing," South told his partner with a touch of asperity. "If he had the ♠J and not the king, his only chance of beating me was to shift to a low spade and hope I misguessed."

My partner said nothing, like a good partner; but at dinner, he pointed out that I had given declarer a chance to make an impossible game.

"You know from my lead of the ◇5 that declarer has at least two diamonds," my partner said. "From the Rule of 11, you know he only has one diamond higher than my five, and it can't be the queen because I would have led the ten from 109852. Lead the ◇7 on the second trick and I'll win and shift to a spade."

He was right, of course, and my satisfaction turned to distress. All I could plead was that I'd had a fixation. Don't let one fix you.

42

This deal arose in a Sectional Swiss and my team lost a swing. My teammates defended well at one table but my partnership goofed up the defense at the other. My partner reproached himself but the fault was mine.

With neither side vulnerable, I held, as East:

♠ A K 5
♡ 2
◇ J 8 2
♣ J 10 6 5 3 2

South dealt and opened 1♠, my partner doubled and North leaped to 4♠. To bid 5♣ would have been speculative at best and I could see us beating up on 4♠. I could score the top trumps and probably a heart ruff and partner would surely contribute a trick or two. So I doubled and all passed.

West led the ♡J.

Dlr: South
Vul: None

North:
♠ 8 7 6 3 2
♡ K 6 4 3
◇ K 10 7 5
♣ —

East:
♠ A K 5
♡ 2
◇ J 8 2
♣ J 10 6 5 3 2

West	North	East	South
			1♠
dbl	4♠	dbl	all pass

Dummy played low, I followed with the deuce and declarer won with the ace. He led the ♠Q, West discarded the ◇9 and I took the king. How should I continue?

I led the ◇2, which looked automatic. It was the old story: 'automatic' plays are the ones that bear scrutiny. South played the ◇4 and my partner took the ace, huddled and returned... the ◇3. That was the end of that. Dummy's king won; South threw a heart. He forced out my other high trump and claimed for +590. The full deal:

	♠ 8 7 6 3 2 ♡ K 6 4 3 ♢ K 10 7 5 ♣ –	
♠ – ♡ J 10 9 7 ♢ A Q 9 6 3 ♣ A Q 9 4	N W E S	♠ A K 5 ♡ 2 ♢ J 8 2 ♣ J 10 6 5 3 2
	♠ Q J 10 9 4 ♡ A Q 8 5 ♢ 4 ♣ K 8 7	

My partner — a good partner he is — fell all over himself taking the blame. He said if he had given his play at the fourth trick more thought, he might have found a heart return. But I put him to an unnecessary guess. On Trick 3, I should have led the ♣J. Dummy would ruff and lead a second trump but then, when I took the ace and led a diamond, my partner would get it right. He would infer that I didn't have a singleton diamond because I didn't shift to it immediately.

At the other table, my teammates bid 4♠ but East judged to save in 5♣. The 'save' almost became a make. Our South led his singleton diamond. Declarer put up dummy's ace and gave himself a chance for the contract when he led the ♡J from dummy. If North had played low, East would have established communication with his hand to finesse in trumps and lose just a heart and a diamond. But North alertly put up the ♡K, cashed the ♢K and gave South a diamond ruff for down one: +100. Still, we lost 10 IMPs when we could have gained five.

Even if your partner is world-class, prevent him from making a mistake if you can.

43

In a local Swiss Teams, my partner is a progressing player. Our opponents are rather more seasoned. After two deals that appear to be flat, I hold, as South:

♠ A J 6
♡ 6
♢ 10 2
♣ A Q 7 6 5 3 2

Both sides are vulnerable. West deals and passes and my partner opens 1NT, 15 to 17. Our bidding system is Stone Age — I wouldn't impose complicated methods on an inexperienced player in a casual partnership — but we did agree to play transfers over 1NT, including a 2♠ response as a transfer to 2NT. So I bid 2♠ and, over his 2NT — I'm thankful he remembered — bid 3♣ to show a good hand with a club suit.

My partner next bids 3NT. He has no special liking for clubs. I could pass — and in a matchpoint game I might — but at IMPs, I think I'll try 5♣. It's possible that 3NT might suffer on a heart lead. I will almost certainly have play for 5♣ and there is a chance that my partner will raise with an appropriate hand.

Everyone passes after 5♣, North after a little thought. West leads the ♡5 and dummy is disappointing:

Dlr: West
Vul: Both

♠ K 10 3
♡ A J 10 4
♢ A Q 5 4
♣ K 10

♠ A J 6
♡ 6
♢ 10 2
♣ A Q 7 6 5 3 2

West	North	East	South
pass	1NT	pass	2♠
pass	2NT	pass	3♣
pass	3NT	pass	5♣
all pass			

"Should I have bid six?" my partner asks.

I suspect he knows he could have. I was willing to undertake an eleven-trick contract and his hand could hardly be better. It looks as though 6♣ is cold if the diamond finesse wins or, failing that, if I locate the ♠Q. Some squeeze possibilities exist as well.

I take the ♡A and cash the ♣K; West discards the ♡3!

Great. Now even our timid 5♣ is not on lock. I ruff a heart — both defenders play low — and try a finesse with the ◊Q. East produces the king and returns a diamond: ten, jack from West, ace from dummy.

This is distressing. My partner thinks he should have bid slam and I'm at risk of going down in game. I'm not sure I can avoid guessing the location of the ♠Q. If West has length in both red suits, I might reach an ending where he has to bare the ♠Q, if he has it… but that looks uncertain. Dummy might be squeezed first and I would still be guessing at the end. I ruff another heart, East following with the king, and take the ♣AQ, leaving:

♠ K 10 3
♡ J
◊ 5
♣ –

♠ A J 6
♡ –
◊ –
♣ 7 6

West has pitched a spade and a diamond on my high trumps and when I exit with a trump to East's jack, West throws a second diamond. Dummy discards a spade. East then produces a high diamond, I ruff and West lets go of a spade. I lead to the ♠K and play another spade; no queen appears. West has the ♡Q left. Is his other card the ♠Q or a low spade? If I don't get this right, my face will be exceedingly red.

West led a heart from Q9753. If his spades were Q752, he might have led a spade. I see no other indication, so I close my eyes and play the jack — and to my relief, it wins. Making five. The full deal:

	North	
	♠ K 10 3 ♡ A J 10 4 ♢ A Q 5 4 ♣ K 10	
♠ 9 7 5 2 ♡ Q 9 7 5 3 ♢ J 9 8 3 ♣ —	N W E S	♠ Q 8 4 ♡ K 8 2 ♢ K 7 6 ♣ J 9 8 4
	♠ A J 6 ♡ 6 ♢ 10 2 ♣ A Q 7 6 5 3 2	

I thought our team might gain a swing with North-South at the other table going down in 6♣, but they bid no more effectively than we did. They stopped in 3NT and scored +660, so we lost 2 IMPs. I think we deserved to lose more.

Declarer faces a taxing issue when the bidding has ended up in the wrong contract. He must focus on making the contract he is in, not the one he wishes he were in. Long after I played this deal, I realized that I could have ensured the contract. All I had to do was play dummy's ♡10 on the first trick. East would win but any return would give me an eleventh trick. If I hadn't still been dwelling on the bidding, I might have found that sure-trick play.

44

Some players have the unfortunate tendency to heap criticism on their partners but even well-intended 'lessons' at the table are dangerous. I can recall times when I was sure my partner had erred — and I told him so — only to conclude, upon reflection, that his play was correct, or at least reasonable.

In a Sectional Open Pairs, my partner is a capable player. Halfway through the session, we have opponents who are unknown to me. On the first board of the round, they played in 4♡, making four. Declarer could have made five with an inspired guess and her partner, obviously the dominant force in the partnership, grumbled under his breath. On the second deal, neither side is vulnerable and, as South, I hold:

♠ K 10 4
♡ 6
◇ A K Q J 10 8 2
♣ A K

East, the dealer, disappoints me by opening 1♡. I double, West offers 1♠, my partner passes and East rebids 2♡.

I have nine cold tricks in diamonds and it is possible that that's all I can take. But my partner might have just a little something useful and our game is not going especially well, so I take a flyer and jump to 5◇. West doubles and all pass. West leads the ♡2.

Dlr: East
Vul: None

♠ Q 6 3
♡ 10 7 4 3
◇ 9 7
♣ 8 7 4 3

♠ K 10 4
♡ 6
◇ A K Q J 10 8 2
♣ A K

West	North	East	South
		1♡	dbl
1♠	pass	2♡	5◇
dbl	all pass		

That's one more good card in dummy than I deserve. I suppose I want too much from life but it's a shame he doesn't have the ♠9 as well. I play low from dummy; East wins with the eight and leads the ♡A. I ruff high and West looks annoyed and discards the ♠5.

I see a chance. I take the ♣AK, lead my ♢2 to dummy's seven, ruff a club high, go back to the ♢9 and ruff the last club. Then I draw West's last trump and lead the ♠K on the tenth trick. The full deal:

	♠ Q 6 3 ♡ 10 7 4 3 ♢ 9 7 ♣ 8 7 4 3	
♠ A J 9 8 5 ♡ 2 ♢ 6 4 3 ♣ J 9 5 2	N W E S	♠ 7 2 ♡ A K Q J 9 8 5 ♢ 5 ♣ Q 10 6
	♠ K 10 4 ♡ 6 ♢ A K Q J 10 8 2 ♣ A K	

West only has spades left. If he ducks, I will lead a second spade and dummy's queen will score; when he takes the ace, he has to lead away from his jack and my ten wins. Making five.

West had to have his say. "Partner," he growled, "if your brains were dynamite, you couldn't blow your nose. Did you think I bid spades so you could lead more hearts?"

Obviously, West thought a spade shift on the second trick would beat 5♢; but he wasn't giving me much credit. I would play the king and West would have to take the ace. If he led, say, a trump next, I would win with the ace, cash the ♣AK, lead a trump to dummy's nine and ruff a club. Then, the run of my trumps would squeeze West in spades and clubs.

Bridge engages a player's ego (like no other game I know). When your partner — this person with whom you have consented to play — makes a mistake, you view it as a reflection of your own ability. It's natural to let everybody know this is not the standard of play to which you are accustomed.

Such behavior reflects insecurity and immaturity. Moreover, my experience has taught me that few players are good enough to tell other players how to play bridge. Even fewer can do it in the emotionally charged atmosphere at the table.

45

Everybody has pet peeves at the table. Mine is self-indulgent and uninformed criticism: hearing a player chew on his partner when the fault for a bad result was his own.

In the first match of a local Swiss Teams, we are opposed by a familiar husband-wife pair. He is a dentist, she a manicurist. They are known to all as 'Tooth and Nail' because that's how they argue. How their partnership survives is a mystery. I think that when they sit down to play, they touch gloves.

This is the opening deal:

Dlr: South
Vul: None

	North	
	♠ A K 7 6 ♡ 10 5 4 ◇ 8 2 ♣ J 5 4 3	
West ♠ Q 10 9 8 5 4 ♡ 7 ◇ K 10 9 ♣ Q 10 9	N / W E / S	**East** ♠ J 2 ♡ Q J 9 3 ◇ Q 6 3 ♣ K 8 7 2
	South ♠ 3 ♡ A K 8 6 2 ◇ A J 7 5 4 ♣ A 6	

Tooth opens 1♡ as South and, as West, I jump to 2♠, preemptive. Nail bids 3♡, my partner passes and Tooth bids 4◇, a try for slam. Nail signs off in 4♡ and, after 40 seconds of study, Tooth passes. I judge to lead the ♣10.

West	North	East	South
			1♡
2♠	3♡	pass	4◇
pass	4♡	all pass	

Dummy plays low and my partner signals encouragement with the eight. Tooth regards the dummy with distaste. He takes the ♣A and cashes dummy's ♠AK, pitching a club. Next, dummy leads a diamond: three, jack and I take my king. When I lead a high spade, my partner discards a diamond and declarer ruffs.

Tooth then cashes the ♡AK, frowning when I show out. He takes the ♢A and ruffs a diamond with dummy's last trump but my partner refuses to overruff. Declarer is stuck in dummy. He ruffs a club and leads a good diamond on the eleventh trick; but East ruffs, cashes his high trump and wins the final trick with the ♣K. Down one.

Then comes the inevitable 'discussion', with Tooth leading the charge.

"How can you bid at the three-level with only 8 points?" he fumes.

"I'm supposed to pass with an ace-king and three-card heart support?" Nail retorts.

"I almost bid a slam," Tooth growls, "and I can't even make a game opposite your garbage."

"Can we please get on with it?" my partner asks politely, while I force myself to remain silent.

Tooth was at fault. Nail's 3♡ was correct; or at least reasonable. Preemption often forces a player to stretch his values to compete and avoid being shut out. South should have been prepared for North to hold a borderline hand. If North had held:

♠ A K 7 6 ♡ K 5 4 ♢ 8 2 ♣ J 5 4 3

she would have to have risked bidding 4♡.

Moreover, 4♡ was unbeatable. After Tooth ruffs the third spade, he should cash just the ♡K, then take the ♢A and ruff a diamond in dummy. Overruffing won't help East. If he discards, declarer comes back to his ♡A and runs the diamonds. He keeps control and loses two trumps and one diamond.

At the other table, my teammates reached 4♡ but the opening lead was a spade. Declarer won and led a diamond to his jack. West took the king and led another spade, doubtless thinking East had no more since declarer hadn't taken an immediate discard. South threw his club loser, crossed to his ♢A and ruffed a diamond. He made the game and we gained 10 IMPs.

Giving lessons at the table is a bad idea, often triggered by an urge to soothe a bruised ego. A hasty analysis may be inaccurate. It may suffer from a lack of objectivity. It is time-consuming and thus an imposition on the other players. It makes it harder to focus on the next deal.

At-the-table criticism is often an exercise in self-justification. Do your partner and yourself a favor. Save the post-mortems for a dispassionate setting after the game when you can criticize yourself as well as him. That's the whole tooth — and nothing but.

46

On a visit to the Birmingham DBC, which I am proud to call my 'home' club, I'm playing in one of the popular '8 Is Enough' team games. (My friend, the late Mary Oshlag, conceived of and implemented the concept.) My team consists of two experts and two inexperienced players; our opponents are configured the same way. How my team should line up to maximize our chances is an interesting question — should the two experts play together? — but I find myself opposite one of the up-and-coming players.

On the opening deal of the second match, I am South, both sides vulnerable, and hold:

♠ 6 5
♡ A 8
♢ 10 7 6 5 4
♣ A 8 6 5

My partner deals and opens 1♢, East passes and I raise to 2♢. I would have a problem if we were playing inverted minor-suit raises — my hand is neither weak nor strong — but in a casual partnership, I insisted that we use no special methods.

West passes and my partner bids 2♠. That bid shows — or ought to show — interest in game, not a fear of playing in diamonds. Since I have a maximum — a fifth diamond and two aces — I must accept. With a stopper in both unbid suits, I jump to 3NT, hoping my partner won't pass if his hand is shapely. But everyone passes and West leads the ♡Q.

Dlr: North
Vul: Both

♠ A K Q 4
♡ 6 5 4 3
♢ K Q J
♣ Q 7

♠ 6 5
♡ A 8
♢ 10 7 6 5 4
♣ A 8 6 5

West	North	East	South
	1♢	pass	2♢
pass	2♠	pass	3NT
all pass			

"I should have opened 1NT," my partner says sheepishly, "but I hoped you would bid notrump or a major so I could raise. I wanted you to play the hand."

"That's a nice compliment," I reply, hoping I can justify his confidence.

East overtakes with the ♡K and I duck. When the ♡2 comes back, I take the ace and lead the ◇Q.

East takes the ace, which is good news. But, unfortunately for me, East is the expert half of the defenders' partnership. He mulls... and shifts to the ♣K! That gives me a second club trick but kills my entry to the diamonds while the suit is still blocked.

I can count only eight tricks — three spades, a heart, two diamonds and two clubs — but I still have a chance. I play low and East leads a second club to dummy's queen. I take the ◇KJ and then the three top spades. On the eleventh trick, I exit with the last spade. Luckily, East must win and lead a club — all he has left — and I win the last two tricks with the ♣A and ◇10. Making three. The full deal:

	North	
	♠ A K Q 4 ♡ 6 5 4 3 ◇ K Q J ♣ Q 7	
West ♠ 7 3 2 ♡ Q J 10 9 7 ◇ 9 2 ♣ J 3 2	N W E S	**East** ♠ J 10 9 8 ♡ K 2 ◇ A 8 3 ♣ K 10 9 4
	♠ 6 5 ♡ A 8 ◇ 10 7 6 5 4 ♣ A 8 6 5	

My partner survived his opening bid but in principle, it is wrong to 'mastermind' — for instance, to distort your bidding to steer the contract into your partner's hand (or into your own hand, if you're a notrump hog). Stick to making your most descriptive bid.

At the other table, North correctly opened 1NT and South liked his aces and five-card suit (even though it was ragged). He raised to 2NT and North went on to the vulnerable game. East led the ♠J and North won, forced out the ◇A and took nine tricks without working up a sweat. It was a hard way for us to achieve a push.

47

This deal was shown to me by a friend who gives playing lessons in the matchpoint games at his club.

"I consider myself a teacher," he told me ruefully, "and I would rather my partners treat our sessions as learning experiences. But I'm getting disillusioned. It seems that many of them are more focused on masterpoints than on improvement. They just expect me to engineer us into winning."

With neither side vulnerable, my friend, as South, held

♠ Q 9 5 4
♡ K 10 6
◇ A 8 5
♣ A 5 3

"East dealt and opened 1◇," he said. "I might have doubled but then my partner would have become declarer."

"It's not clear to double with your hand anyway," I observed. "You have a bunch of losers; your hand is better for defense."

"I passed," my friend said, nodding, "West raised to 2◇ and two passes followed. If I'd been playing with you, I would have reopened with a double; but I still couldn't afford to let my partner get his hands on the dummy. So I bid 2♠."

I shuddered.

"I know, I know." My friend sighed. "Everybody passed and West led the ◇3."

Dlr: East
Vul: None

♠ K J 2
♡ 7 5 2
◇ 7 4 2
♣ K Q 10 6

♠ Q 9 5 4
♡ K 10 6
◇ A 8 5
♣ A 5 3

West	North	East	South
		1◇	pass
2◇	pass	pass	2♠(!)
all pass			

"It was a better dummy than I deserved," my friend said. "At least my partner was aware that I had bid some of his points when I balanced and didn't raise me to 4♠.

"East played the ♢Q and I ducked. He returned the ♢10 to my ace and West followed with the six. I led a trump to dummy's king and East took the ace — he might have done better to duck — and led the ♢9. West's jack won and he shifted to a heart, which wasn't best defense either. East took the ace and led a heart to my king.

"I knew that East had started with only three diamonds. He must have had four hearts and four spades or else West would have responded in a major. Moreover, with 4-3-3-3 or 3-4-3-3 shape, East probably would have opened 1♣."

My friend led a trump to the jack and a trump back to... his nine. When West discarded, declarer drew the last trump, took the ♣KA and led a third club to... dummy's ten. The ♣Q won the thirteenth trick; making three! The full deal:

West	North	East
	♠ K J 2 ♡ 7 5 2 ♢ 7 4 2 ♣ K Q 10 6	
♠ 7 6 ♡ J 9 3 ♢ K J 6 3 ♣ J 8 4 2	N W E S	♠ A 10 8 3 ♡ A Q 8 4 ♢ Q 10 9 ♣ 9 7
	♠ Q 9 5 4 ♡ K 10 6 ♢ A 8 5 ♣ A 5 3	

"I did my job," my friend told me, "and my pupil was happy with the masterpoints we won. I just hope he also learned something about drawing inferences as declarer."

Players have different motives for retaining a professional partner. To pay for the pleasure of seeing the game played competently, to be a part of a well-played session, is fine. To pay a capable pro for the purpose of improving your game in the fire of competition is fine. To pay someone solely to generate masterpoints — to compensate for one's own inadequacies — is, in my opinion, delusional.

48

I was relaxing in the lounge of my bridge club with a friend — he happens to be a professor of English — when a player came in from the afternoon Swiss Teams and wrote down this hand on a napkin:

♠ A 9 7
♡ 10 6 2
◊ Q 10 9 4 3 2
♣ 8

"Only our side was vulnerable," he told us. "My partner held this hand as South. I dealt and opened 1♣, East doubled and my partner bid 1◊. West competed with 1♠ and I raised to 3◊. Then East jumped to 4♠. What would you have done as South?"

We considered the matter. South seemed to have good defense against 4♠ — a club lead would surely result in at least one ruff — but the North hand was marked with a spade shortage, so 5◊ might be cold.

"My partner bid 5◊," we heard, "but I wouldn't have wanted to be in that contract with a ten-foot pole."

"How's that again?" The professor frowned.

"When East bid 4♠, my partner should have let dead dogs sleep."

"Beg your pardon?"

The full deal had been:

	North ♠ — ♡ A J 7 5 ◊ J 8 7 6 ♣ A K 7 4 3	
♠ J 10 8 4 2 ♡ 4 3 ◊ K 5 ♣ Q 9 5 2	N / W E / S	♠ K Q 6 5 3 ♡ K Q 9 8 ◊ A ♣ J 10 6
	South ♠ A 9 7 ♡ 10 6 2 ◊ Q 10 9 4 3 2 ♣ 8	

West	North	East	South
	1♣	dbl	1◊
1♠	3◊	4♠	5◊
all pass			

"In 5♢," North told us, "my partner was between a rock and the deep blue sea. He couldn't succeed by hook or ladder. West led a heart and partner took the ♡A, sat there like a sore thumb, cashed the ♣AK to discard a heart and led the ♢J, hoping East might cover with Kx. But East had the singleton ace and South had to swallow the bullet. He went down, losing a heart and two trumps, for -100."

The professor threw a wet towel on the discussion.

"Getting down to brass roots," he said, "South should have grabbed the bull by the tail and looked him in the eye."

My friend was quite right. If South plays well, the shoe will be on the other horse. South discards a heart on the top clubs, ruffs a club, ruffs a spade and ruffs a club. He ruffs a spade and leads the good fifth club.

If East ruffs with his ace, South throws his last heart, losing only two trump tricks. So East discards, South discards his last heart and West ruffs low and leads another heart. South ruffs and leads a trump, bringing down the AK together.

"It's as easy as falling off a piece of cake," I offered.

"Maybe so," North shrugged, "but if my partner had found that line of play, you could have knocked me over with a fender."

At the other table, I learned later, the auction was slightly different. North opened 1♣ again — I hope that nobody would open 1♢ on that hand, though I've seen players do exactly that — but East overcalled 1♠ instead of doubling, getting his five-card suit mentioned. South couldn't act and West raised preemptively to 3♠.

North didn't think he had enough to double but East unwisely went to 4♠ and South found a good penalty double. He led his singleton club and the defense took two high clubs, a club ruff and the major-suit aces for +300 and a 9-IMP gain.

49

In a Sectional Open Pairs, both sides are vulnerable and as South, the dealer, I pick up:

♠ —
♡ K Q 10 8 7 6 4
◇ Q 10 3
♣ A K 3

I open 1♡, West doubles and my partner raises to 2♡. Many players treat a single raise over a double as a nuisance action, showing trump support but little else. Personally, I dislike bidding on nothing and would have a trick or two to raise whether West had doubled or not.

Since my hand is so shapely, I expect the auction to turn competitive; sure enough, East leaps to 4♠. I certainly can't let them play that; both 4♠ and 5♡ may be cold. The Law of Total Tricks enters my thoughts. We probably have ten hearts and I'm guessing that East-West have ten spades. If the LOTT is accurate here, twenty tricks should be available in heart and spade contracts. It will be right, quoth the Law, for me to bid 5♡. If I go down one, the opponents could have made their game.

It's possible that we might even make a slam. My partner could produce a dummy such as:

♠ 5 4 3 ♡ A 9 3 ◇ K 9 8 2 ♣ 7 6 5

and I could guess the location of the ◇J to make twelve tricks. But since partners never have ideal cards, I decline to issue a try for slam with a 5♣ cuebid: I just bid 5♡ and everyone passes.

West leads the ♠K and, when dummy hits, I see that I may have misjudged.

Dlr: South
Vul: Both

♠ A 9 4
♡ J 9 3
◇ 8 7 5 4 2
♣ Q 10

♠ —
♡ K Q 10 8 7 6 4
◇ Q 10 3
♣ A K 3

West	North	East	South
			1♡
dbl	2♡	4♠	5♡
all pass			

The contract has three losers; nevertheless, I see a slim chance. West's opening lead was not a top diamond, so if he had four diamonds, East has a singleton king or ace. I throw a diamond on the ♠A, ruff a spade and take my three top clubs, pitching dummy's last spade. Next, I lead the ♡Q. West pauses, then takes his ace and exits with a trump. East discards a spade.

Upon winning, I mentally cross my fingers and lead a diamond. As it happens, the full deal is:

North:
♠ A 9 4
♡ J 9 3
◇ 8 7 5 4 2
♣ Q 10

West:
♠ K Q 6
♡ A 5
◇ A J 9 6
♣ J 9 7 4

East:
♠ J 10 8 7 5 3 2
♡ 2
◇ K
♣ 8 6 5 2

South:
♠ —
♡ K Q 10 8 7 6 4
◇ Q 10 3
♣ A K 3

When East takes the ◇K, he has to concede a ruff-and-sluff and my last diamond goes away. Making five.

My competitive judgment and the LOTT were both slightly out of whack. My estimate of twenty trumps was correct but 4♠ would fail — we would take two clubs and a club ruff, plus the ♠A — and 5♡ should fail also. On the second trump, East could lose nothing by discarding his ♢K and West would get two diamonds.

The LOTT is most accurate on partscore deals and often breaks down at higher levels. In a deal such as this one, it is often better to bid one more for luck and get to be declarer. Moreover, the LOTT assumes perfect play and defense — but deals are played at the table, not in a realm of perfection.

50

In a Sectional Compact Knockout, we are opposed by a capable team. My partner is less experienced but progressing. Only the opponents are vulnerable and, as South, I hold:

♠ 7 4 3 2
♡ A K 9 8 3
◇ 10 9 7 4
♣ –

West, the dealer, opens 1♡ and my partner ponders and jumps to 2NT: 'Unusual' for the minors. East bids 3♠ and I must now judge.

If my partner has values in clubs and a singleton heart, we might beat 3♠ and mangle 4♠. If most of his high-card strength is in diamonds, we might still beat 4♠ but we might make 5◇.

The Law of Total Tricks suggests that I go no higher than 4◇. Assume we have a nine-card diamond fit and they have a nine-card spade fit. Then, if I can make 4◇, we can beat 3♠. But the LOTT can break down at high levels and here, I don't know where my partner's values lie. Moreover, I can't be sure how many spades the opponents have.

I think maybe my correct bid is 4◇, consulting my partner; but, instead, I decide to force the opponents to make the last guess: I jump to 5◇. West doubles and everyone passes.

West leads the ◇A and my partner proudly displays a dummy I was hardly expecting.

Dlr: West
Vul: E-W

North:
♠ A
♡ 10
◇ K Q J 8 5 3
♣ 10 9 8 6 4

South:
♠ 7 4 3 2
♡ A K 9 8 3
◇ 10 9 7 4
♣

West	North	East	South
1♡	2NT(!)	3♠	5◇
dbl	all pass		

Six good diamonds, no points in clubs! His 2NT was unusual as well as Unusual. Few players would have treated the hand that way: most would have bid 2♢ or 3♢. An Unusual 2NT may be based on 11 minor-suit cards but then the clubs will be longer.

East follows to the ♢A and West leads another trump. Dummy wins; East discards a spade.

I can count ten tricks: five trumps in dummy, two club ruffs in my hand, two high hearts and the ♠A. If I proceed with a crossruff, I may fall a trick short. But I see an option. I have no more top losers, so I can afford to concede one more trick; I lead dummy's ♡10 and let it ride. West wins with the jack and leads a spade; I take the ace, ruff a club, cash the ♡AK and lead the ♡9 for a ruffing finesse through West. His queen covers and I ruff in dummy, ruff a club and score the ♡8 for my eleventh trick. The full deal:

West	North / South	East
	♠ A ♡ 10 ♢ K Q J 8 5 3 ♣ 10 9 8 6 4	
♠ J 9 6 ♡ Q J 7 6 4 ♢ A 6 ♣ K Q 7	N W E S	♠ K Q 10 8 5 ♡ 5 2 ♢ 2 ♣ A J 5 3 2
	♠ 7 4 3 2 ♡ A K 9 8 3 ♢ 10 9 7 4 ♣ —	

At the other table, the auction started 1♡-2♢-2♠. South jumped to 5♢ again, with rather more of an excuse than I had; but after two passes, East judged that his partner's pass over 5♢ implied spade tolerance. So, East bid 5♠. South doubled and all passed. The defenders took the ♡AK, the ♠A and a club ruff but that was all they managed. They were +500, so our +550 was enough to gain 2 IMPs.

51

In a Bracketed Knockout event, both sides are vulnerable and, as South, I hold:

♠ 7
♡ Q J 9 7 6
◊ A Q 10 7 4
♣ K 4

East deals and opens 1♠ and I must choose a call. I certainly must act with this much shape and high-card strength. A double would be ill-advised; with a two-suited hand, I need to start showing my suits.

We are playing Michaels, so a 2♠ cuebid to show hearts and a minor is available. The tendency — or a tendency — is to use Michaels on hands with playing strength but limited defense: a hand suitable for a sacrifice, such as:

♠7 ♡K Q J 7 6 ◊Q J 10 7 4 2 ♣4

or on a big hand such as:

♠7 ♡A K J 7 6 ◊A K 7 4 2 ♣K 4

with which the Michaels bidder will act again. In-between hands, such as mine, overcall 2♡ and hope to bid the minor suit later.

I could try 2♡ but we are vulnerable at IMPs and if I use Michaels, I don't think my partner will play me for a hand weaker than the one I hold. Bidding diamonds at the three-level, even if I get that chance, would make me uneasy, so I start with 2♠.

West passes and my partner bids 2NT, asking me to bid my minor. When I follow through with 3◊, he raises to 4◊. I have no idea whether I should go on — this is not an everyday auction — but a vulnerable game is at stake. So I bid 5◊, hoping for the best, and everyone passes.

West leads the ♠10 and I see that we have reached game with 19 points, two of which are wasted.

Dlr: East
Vul: Both

♠ Q 6 5 3
♡ 10
◇ J 9 6 3 2
♣ A 8 6

♠ 7
♡ Q J 9 7 6
◇ A Q 10 7 4
♣ K 4

West	North	East	South
		1♠	2♠
pass	2NT	pass	3◇
pass	4◇	pass	5◇
all pass			

The ♠10 wins and West continues with the nine. East overtakes with the jack and I ruff.

The contract has a chance. East opened the bidding, so the trump finesse should win. If he has the singleton king, a crossruff might bring in 11 tricks, but I can't count on that. I will probably need to establish my fifth heart and doing so will require sufficient entries to my hand. It may not do to lead a club to dummy and draw trumps with a finesse if East has K-x. So on the third trick, I lead a heart.

West rises with the ♡K and leads a third spade; I ruff, ruff a heart in dummy and lead a trump to my queen, winning as West follows low. I take the ◇A, ruff another heart, ruff dummy's last spade with my last trump and ruff a heart with dummy's last trump, dropping East's ace. Then I can claim the last three tricks with the ♣AK and my good heart, making five.

If I draw trumps prematurely, I fail. The full deal:

	♠ Q 6 5 3 ♡ 10 ♢ J 9 6 3 2 ♣ A 8 6	
♠ 10 9 2 ♡ K 4 3 ♢ 5 ♣ Q 9 7 5 3 2	N W E S	♠ A K J 8 4 ♡ A 8 5 2 ♢ K 8 ♣ J 10
	♠ 7 ♡ Q J 9 7 6 ♢ A Q 10 7 4 ♣ K 4	

At the other table, South chose the 2♡ overcall I rejected. West was willing to raise spades to the two-level, North couldn't act and my teammate in East took a rosy view, no doubt eyeing the vulnerability, and bid 4♠. What he expected to do with all his heart losers is unclear. All passed and the contract went a quiet down two for -200. Still, my team gained 9 IMPs.

52

In a Sectional Swiss Teams, neither side is vulnerable and, as South, the dealer, I pick up:

♠ K 7
♡ A 7 3
◇ K Q 10 9 6 5
♣ 7 5

When I open 1◇, West overcalls 2◇, a Michaels cuebid, showing length in both majors. If I were West, I would have either a good playing hand with limited defense or a rock-solid hand. With a middling hand such as:

♠ A Q 10 6 3 ♡ K Q 10 6 5 ◇ 4 ♣ K 4

I would overcall 1♠, intending to bid hearts later. But players embrace their own styles and this West may have a hand with which Michaels wouldn't occur to me.

North doubles. What he has is also unknown but his double tells me that the deal belongs to us. We may or may not bid a game; but we won't let the opponents play undoubled if they buy the contract. East and I pass, West rescues himself to 2♡ and two passes follow. My partner expects me to act, so I rebid 3◇.

After West passes, North bids 4♣. I still don't know where we are headed but partner sounds hungry. My ♠K may be a worthless card but, since I haven't shown any sign of life so far, I think I can afford to cuebid 4♡. My partner comes back with 5♣. Maybe I ought to pass; he may have clubs. I don't know. I try 5◇. Surely North wouldn't bid this way with nothing in diamonds. If we can make a high club contract, maybe we will do just as well in diamonds.

My partner huddles... and extracts the 6◇ card from his bidding box. Everyone passes. I hope we haven't bid a no-play slam. West leads the ♡Q.

"I think you have to have a high spade," my partner says as he tables the dummy, "but if you go down, I'll take the blame."

Dlr: South
Vul: None

♠ 9 4 3 2
♡ K 6 2
◇ A J 3
♣ A K Q

♠ K 7
♡ A 7 3
◇ K Q 10 9 6 5
♣ 7 5

West	North	East	South
			1◇
2◇	dbl	pass	pass
2♡	pass	pass	3◇
pass	4♣	pass	4♡
pass	5♣	pass	5◇
pass	6◇	all pass	

I can count eleven tricks; but leading up to the ♠K will be futile. I think my only chance is to put pressure on West. I win the first heart with the ace and cash the ◇AJ. West discards a spade, so I cash dummy's top clubs, pitching a heart, and run the rest of my trumps. The position as I lead my last trump is:

North:
♠ 9 4
♡ K 6
◇ –
♣ –

West:
♠ A Q
♡ Q J
◇ –
♣ –

East:
♠ 10 8
♡ 8
◇ –
♣ J

South:
♠ K 7
♡ 7
◇ 5 (led)
♣ –

West must give up the ghost. If he throws a heart, dummy wins two heart tricks. When he throws the ♠Q, I discard dummy's low heart, lead a low spade to fell the ace and win the last two tricks. The full deal:

	North	
	♠ 9 4 3 2 ♡ K 6 2 ♢ A J 3 ♣ A K Q	
♠ A Q J 6 5 ♡ Q J 10 9 5 ♢ 4 ♣ 9 4	N W E S	♠ 10 8 ♡ 8 4 ♢ 8 7 2 ♣ J 10 8 6 3 2
	♠ K 7 ♡ A 7 3 ♢ K Q 10 9 6 5 ♣ 7 5	

At the other table, my teammate in West overcalled 1♠ on his first turn. After that, South kept his foot firmly on the brake and North-South stopped in 4NT, making six on the lead of the ♠Q.

At my table, West's 2♢ cuebid was certainly beyond reproach. I might have chosen it myself. Still, I am continually struck by how intervention with a weak hand can backfire by giving the opponents useful information in judging the bidding or the play or both. If West doesn't act, North-South might reach 6♢ but I doubt that South would make it.

Because constructive bidding has become more accurate over the past few decades, players are increasingly likely to focus on obstructing their opponents' auctions. In my opinion, the case for silence is stronger than they believe.

53

In a Bracketed Knockout Teams, both sides are vulnerable. East, the dealer, opens 1♠ and, as South, I must choose an action with:

♠ 8 3
♡ Q 10 9 7 4
◊ A K 9 7 3
♣ A

For some players, my hand would be suitable for a Michaels cuebid, showing length in both hearts and one of the minors. I wouldn't criticize that action but, as I have mentioned, I adhere to the classical approach where Michaels is appropriate with either: a weak, offensively oriented hand potentially suitable for a sacrifice; or a huge hand. With in-between hands such as this, I overcall 2♡.

West passes, my partner raises to 3♡ and East passes. I should have play for game if North has good trump support and little else. Of course, he might have three low hearts and a bunch of club honors and then we may be overboard in 3♡; but I can't afford to miss a vulnerable game at IMPs. So, I bid 4♡ and am relieved when nobody doubles.

West leads the ♠2.

Dlr: East
Vul: Both

North:
♠ K 10
♡ K J 8 3
◊ J 10 5 4
♣ Q 8 6

South:
♠ 8 3
♡ Q 10 9 7 4
◊ A K 9 7 3
♣ A

West	North	East	South
		1♠	2♡
pass	3♡	pass	4♡
all pass			

North's ♠K might as well be the four but, I suppose, he still had his 3♡ bid. I play the ten from dummy and East takes the queen and ace and shifts to the ♡A and a second heart. West follows and I win in dummy. They have drawn trumps for me, so now everything depends on whether I bring in the diamonds.

I wonder whether I can do any card-placing. East doesn't need the ◊Q to have an opening bid; he could have the ♠AQ, ♡A and ♣K. It occurs to me that I can lead the ♣Q from dummy as a 'discovery play'. If East has the king, he will surely cover. If he plays low, I can place West with the king and, hence, East with the ◊Q since West would have raised to 2♠ with the ♠J, ◊Q and ♣K.

When I lead the ♣Q, East covers. Next, I take the ◊A and both defenders play low. No clues from the bidding are compelling. If East had:

♠A Q 7 5 4 ♡A 2 ◊Q 8 6 ♣K 10 3

he might have opened 1NT; but I think that inference is too slender to stake the contract on.

But I can rely on a stronger inference — from the defense. Suppose West had a low singleton diamond. He knew his partner had a good hand, maybe with some aces. How would West have defended? As a matter of fact, if West had a stiff diamond, they could have beaten me easily. West leads his singleton; I win and lead a trump. East takes the ace and gives West a diamond ruff; then, they take two spades.

Since nothing like that happened, I don't think West does have a singleton. I bang down the ◊K and the full deal is:

West	North / South	East
	♠ K 10 ♡ K J 8 3 ◊ J 10 5 4 ♣ Q 8 6	
♠ J 9 6 2 ♡ 6 5 ◊ Q 2 ♣ J 9 5 4 2	N W E S	♠ A Q 7 5 4 ♡ A 2 ◊ 8 6 ♣ K 10 7 3
	♠ 8 3 ♡ Q 10 9 7 4 ◊ A K 9 7 3 ♣ A	

Some inferences are valid only against experts whose play can be trusted implicitly. The inference I drew here would have been reliable even against a novice West; all players are attracted to leading singletons.

Players often tell me that they are reluctant to draw inferences from the play because their opponents can't be trusted to operate logically. That argument is specious. Always assume your opponent has played correctly. If he hasn't and you go down in a contract you could have made, you can laugh it off. You can tell yourself that you made a thoughtful play that failed because your opponent was out to lunch. But if you assume that your opponent has erred when in fact he hasn't, you will have only yourself to blame.

54

I'm playing in a friendly after-dinner home team game. In a tournament, I make it a practice to eat a light meal before a session; but this evening, my hostess has served lobster omelets, so all bets are off. On an early deal, both sides are vulnerable and stuffed and I hold:

♠ A J 4
♡ K J 10 9 8 5 2
♢ 6
♣ K 4

East deals and opens 1♢ and I overcall 1♡. My hand is way too strong for a preempt and I can't assume the deal belongs to the opponents. West passes and my partner advances with 1NT. We happen to have an agreement that a 1NT response to an overcall is forcing, like a forcing 1NT response to an opening bid. I know of no expert pairs who use this treatment but that doesn't make it a bad idea. Since our style is to overcall soundly, we find it useful to have a bid to keep the auction going. East passes.

A vulnerable game beckons and I could jump to 4♡. But North probably has some diamond strength that would be wasted when playing in hearts, so I give him some room and just bid 3♡. He ponders and raises to 4♡, passed out. West leads the ♢Q.

Dlr: East
Vul: Both

♠ 10 9 2
♡ A Q
♢ K 5 2
♣ J 8 6 5 2

♠ A J 4
♡ K J 10 9 8 5 2
♢ 6
♣ K 4

West	North	East	South
		1♢	1♡
pass	1NT	pass	3♡
pass	4♡	all pass	

North's ♢K is indeed worthless; maybe he should have bid 3NT on his second turn, though I don't know that I would have left him there. West's ♢Q wins and he continues with the ♢J. I ruff. East figures to hold the ♣A and at least one spade honor for his opening bid, so I can see ten tricks: seven hearts, the ♣K and two spades. I just have to take care when managing my dummy entries.

I lead a trump to dummy on the third trick. Since I will probably need to finesse twice in spades, I need to attack that suit next. If instead I lead a club toward my king, East may take the ace and lead anything other than a spade and I won't be able to take two spade finesses. So on Trick 4, I call for dummy's ♠2 — not the ten: three from East, jack, queen. West leads a third diamond and I ruff, lead a trump to dummy and run the ♠10, which holds. Then I can lead a club toward my king for +620. The full deal:

	North	
	♠ 10 9 2 ♡ A Q ♢ K 5 2 ♣ J 8 6 5 2	
West ♠ Q 8 6 5 ♡ 7 3 ♢ Q J 7 4 ♣ 10 9 3	N W E S	**East** ♠ K 7 3 ♡ 6 4 ♢ A 10 9 8 3 ♣ A Q 7
	♠ A J 4 ♡ K J 10 9 8 5 2 ♢ 6 ♣ K 4	

If I'm careless with my entries, I go down. If, for instance, I start the spades by leading the ten, I have to win the second spade finesse in my hand and will not be able to lead toward my ♣K.

At the other table, East opened 1NT, showing 12 to 14 high-card points, and South jumped to 3♡. After West passed, North had a shot at 3NT and South showed admirable faith by passing.

After a diamond opening lead, North would have had nine tricks; but my teammate in East found the inspired lead of a spade. Declarer had to take dummy's ace; if he ducked, West would win and shift to the ♢Q. North then peeled off seven heart tricks... but East-West held the high ground. East's last five cards were the ♠K7, ♢A10 and ♣A. The defense took the rest for +100 and we gained 12 IMPs.

55

Before I began to focus on writing, when I was a competitor, my approach to bidding was founded on sound initial actions. My overcalls were, in fact, known for being rock-solid.

Once, at a Regional, with both sides vulnerable, my right-hand opponent opened 1♡, I overcalled 2♣ and the next player doubled for penalty. All passed, a heart was led and my partner (my old friend Allen Hawkins) displayed a dummy with a singleton club and one queen. Our opponents, two women, couldn't help but chuckle.

"Lady," the Hawk told the opening leader, "you'll need to defend double-dummy to beat this."

I went down one; the opponents were cold for 4♠.

In a Sectional Open Pairs, I have a capable partner and we are opposed by a seeded pair. Only our side is vulnerable and, as South, I hold:

♠ 8 5 4
♡ A K Q J 10 5
◊ J 4
♣ K Q

East, the dealer, opens 1♣ and I 'risk' a 1♡ overcall. If I get doubled, I should have play for seven tricks! West passes and my partner tries 2◊.

Pairs use different approaches in 'advancing' partner's simple overcall, depending somewhat on how light they are willing to overcall. Some pairs play a new suit as forcing at the one-level, not forcing at the two-level. In our style, based on sound overcalls, we treat a new suit at the two-level as not quite forcing but encouraging. Well, I am encouraged enough to jump to 4♡. All pass and West leads the ♣J.

Dlr: East
Vul: Both

♠ K Q 3
♡ 6 3
◊ K Q 10 9 3
♣ 7 4 2

♠ 8 5 4
♡ A K Q J 10 5
◊ J 4
♣ K Q

West	North	East	South
		1♣	1♡
pass	2◇	pass	4♡
all pass			

East takes the ♣A — I follow with the queen — and ponders. If he leads another club, I'll be safe. I can win, draw trumps, knock out the ◇A and lose only one more trick to the ♠A. But East finds a good defense; he shifts to a low spade. West's nine forces out the queen and my late entry to dummy is no more.

I may be fated to go down but I see a chance if East started with only three clubs. I draw trumps, cash the ♣K and lead the ◇J. West signals with the deuce and, when I overtake with the queen, East plays low. I ruff dummy's last club and lead a second diamond to dummy; the full deal is:

West	North / South	East
	♠ K Q 3 ♡ 6 3 ◇ K Q 10 9 3 ♣ 7 4 2	
♠ 10 9 2 ♡ 7 4 ◇ 8 5 2 ♣ J 10 9 6 3	N W E S	♠ A J 7 6 ♡ 9 8 2 ◇ A 7 6 ♣ A 8 5
	♠ 8 5 4 ♡ A K Q J 10 5 ◇ J 4 ♣ K Q	

East takes the ◇A and has only spades and a diamond left. He can only cash his ♠A to hold me to ten tricks.

I wondered whether I could have made my game if East had had four clubs. When I checked using a double-dummy solver, I found that the run of my trumps would have strip-squeezed East into conceding the contract. I think I should have preferred that line of play.

As to the auction, I think it might be worth considering, given a sound overcalling style, treating a 1NT advance as forcing, like a forcing 1NT response to an opening bid.

56

In a Sectional Flighted Pairs, I have a partner who shares some of my quaint views on bidding. (As the saying goes, everybody is entitled to my opinion.) Neither side is vulnerable and, as South, I hold:

♠ K Q 4 3
♡ 9 2
◇ A K 4 3
♣ J 9 2

My partner deals and opens 1♣. I respond 1♠ — some players would respond 1◇ — and he raises to 2♠.

My hand is worth game and with a partner whose 2♠ absolutely promised four-card support, I would bid 4♠. But our partnership style is to raise a major-suit response with three-card support in a suitable hand and partner would be especially willing to raise me after 1♣-1♠, inferring that I would often hold at least five spades since I hadn't responded in a red suit.

How should I proceed? We might do well in 3NT if I could get us there; North could hold:

♠J 6 5 ♡A K Q ◇6 5 ♣A 10 8 6 4

If I held:

♠Q 7 4 3 ♡A 10 5 ◇K 4 3 ♣Q 9 2

I could bid 2NT next and respect his signoff in 3♣ or 3♠.

With:

♠Q 7 4 3 ♡A Q 5 ◇K 4 3 ♣K 9 2

I would bid 3NT, offering a choice of games.

With:

♠K Q 4 3 ♡9 2 ◇A Q 4 3 ♣8 7 6

I could try 3◇.

With:

♠K Q 4 3 ♡9 2 ◇8 7 6 2 ♣A Q 3

I could bid 3♣, though a case exists for treating that bid as not forcing. (Many pairs employ artificial continuations after opener raises a major-suit response.)

As it is, I think my spades are strong enough to play opposite a three-card raise and I don't want to give the defenders any more information about my hand, so I jump to 4♠. Everyone passes and West leads the ♡K.

Dlr: North
Vul: None

♠ A 5 2
♡ 7 6
♢ 8 5 2
♣ A K Q 10 4

♠ K Q 4 3
♡ 9 2
♢ A K 4 3
♣ J 9 2

West	North	East	South
	1♣	pass	1♠
pass	2♠	pass	4♠
all pass			

Some players would have rebid 2♣ with that North hand; we might have reached 4♠ anyway after I then bid diamonds and North took a spade preference. Our actual auction was simpler and less revealing and we reached the best game. East-West could have cashed at least five hearts against 3NT and 5♣ would require a 3-3 spade break or an unlikely squeeze.

East signals with the eight on the first heart and West continues with the ♡4 to East's jack. Then East shifts to the ♢9, won by my ace.

I can see ten tricks: two diamonds, five clubs and at least three trumps. All I have to do is take them. If I cash my top trumps, I can claim an overtrick if trumps break 3-3; but if they break 4-2, I will be in the soup. If I concede the fourth trump, the defenders will cash hearts; if instead I start with the clubs, a defender may ruff the third club, cutting me off from dummy and leaving me with at least one diamond loser. So I must make sure of being able to use dummy's clubs.

How about taking the ♠KQ, saving the ♠A as a late entry to dummy, then starting the clubs? That might work but I can see brewing myself a pot of trouble by leaving the defenders with two trumps.

An overtrick would be nice but I think I should play as safe as I can to make four; +620 will surely be a good result. On the fourth trick, I play a low trump from both hands. East wins and leads the ♦Q and I win and cash the ♠A. When both defenders follow, I draw trumps with the K-Q and run the clubs in peace. My low diamonds go away and I end up with ten tricks. The full deal:

	North	
	♠ A 5 2 ♥ 7 6 ♦ 8 5 2 ♣ A K Q 10 4	
West ♠ 10 6 ♥ K Q 10 4 3 ♦ J 10 7 6 ♣ 8 6	N W E S	East ♠ J 9 8 7 ♥ A J 8 5 ♦ Q 9 ♣ 7 5 3
	♠ K Q 4 3 ♥ 9 2 ♦ A K 4 3 ♣ J 9 2	

East's best defense was to lead another heart on the third trick, giving me a useless ruff-and-sluff, but as the cards lay, I could still succeed. I could pitch a diamond, ruff in dummy and take the top trumps. When they broke 4-2, I could start on the clubs and get rid of my last low diamond as East ruffed.

Our matchpoint result for +620 was good. At many tables, North-South strayed into 5♣ or even 3NT and went minus. A few pairs obtained a plus in a partscore. Pairs who were +140 in spades scored above average.

As to North's bid of 2♠, my experience suggests that raising a major with decent three-card support — and a hand that looks good for suit play — is a winning tactic. Auctions are easier when a trump suit is suggested early. True, you will occasionally get stuck in a poor 4-3 fit; but then you might not have had a better spot anywhere else.

57

This is a deal in which I pitched 12 IMPs by playing too quickly — a common fault I should know to avoid. In a Sectional Swiss Teams, both sides are vulnerable and as West, the dealer, I hold:

♠ 8 5
♡ K 7 4
◇ A 10 7 4
♣ A K 10 8

What to open on a balanced hand with 4-4 in the minors is a topic of expert contention. Some experts routinely open 1◇, others 1♣. Many choose influenced by suit quality.

Although opening 1◇ may gain if the auction turns competitive (opener would have an awkward second call, for example, after 1♣-2♠-Dbl-Pass), my preference is to start with 1♣ to make it easier to locate a big fit in either minor. I certainly wouldn't open 1◇ and bid 2♣ over a major-suit response, suggesting a two-suiter when I don't have one: I would rebid 1NT over a 1♠ response or raise a 1♡ response to 2♡. The 1◇-then-2♣ plan would fail to limit my strength to a minimum — a dangerous course — and might result in a silly contract on a 4-2 diamond fit.

My clubs are significantly stronger here, so I open 1♣ with no guilt. As it happens, I need not have worried about describing my hand. Two passes follow. South doubles, North responds 1◇ and South jumps to 2♠. North ponders and raises to 3♠ and South goes on to 4♠, passed out. I lead the ♣K.

Dlr: West
Vul: Both

North:
♠ 7 3
♡ Q 10 8
◇ K Q 9 5
♣ 7 6 4 3

West:
♠ 8 5
♡ K 7 4
◇ A 10 7 4
♣ A K 10 8

West	North	East	South
1♣	pass	pass	dbl
pass	1◇	pass	2♠
pass	3♠	pass	4♠
all pass			

Dummy follows with the three, my partner plays the nine and declarer contributes the five. I promptly continue with the ♣A, dropping declarer's jack, and a third club: six, queen, ruff. South takes the ♠AK, and East follows with the deuce and jack. Declarer then tables the ♢J.

If my partner has a trump trick, we will beat 4♠ even if I don't take my ♢A now — and never get it; I will still score the ♡K. But if declarer's trumps are solid, we need a heart trick as well as a diamond. If he holds:

♠AKQ9642 ♡A2 ♢J3 ♣J5

I need to duck the ♢J. After some fruitless thought, I play South for 7-3-1-2 shape: I take the ♢A and lead a fourth club. South ruffs and, inevitably, produces a second diamond. He discards a heart on a high diamond in dummy and claims. The full deal:

West	North / South	East
	♠ 7 3	
	♡ Q 10 8	
	♢ K Q 9 5	
	♣ 7 6 4 3	
♠ 8 5	N	♠ J 2
♡ K 7 4	W E	♡ 9 6 5 3 2
♢ A 10 7 4	S	♢ 8 6 2
♣ A K 10 8		♣ Q 9 2
	♠ A K Q 10 9 6 4	
	♡ A J	
	♢ J 3	
	♣ J 5	

I apologized to my partner for misguessing but he pointed out that I wouldn't have beaten the contract by ducking the ♢J. Declarer would have overtaken with dummy's queen, ruffed the last club and led the ♢3. Then when I won, I would have had to give dummy the ♢K or led a heart away from my king.

In fact, my error had come earlier. On the second trick, I could have led my ♣8 to partner's queen and he could have shifted to a heart, establishing the setting trick for my king while I still had the ♢A. On the bidding, East was rather more likely to hold ♣ Q92 than doubleton ♣ 92, so I should have gotten this one right.

58

In a Sectional Swiss Teams, we have won our first two matches — one with a blitz — and are facing tough opposition in the match before the lunch break. After two indecisive deals, I hold, as South:

♠ J 8 7 4 2
♡ A J 9 8 3 2
◇ —
♣ 5 4

Only the opponents are vulnerable and my partner deals and opens 1♣. East passes. We could be cold for a slam but I must tread carefully; I could just as easily be facing a nasty misfit.

In some circumstances, I might handle a 6-5 hand by bidding the five-card suit first. As dealer with:

♠ A K J 6 4 ♡ Q 10 6 5 3 2 ◇ K 5 ♣ —

I would consider opening 1♠. The hand would lack the high-card strength to open 1♡ and reverse into spades next. (In some partnerships, using a Two-over-One style, opener might be able to open 1♡ and rebid 2♠ after a two-level response without promising extra strength.)

Here, my hand is so weak in high cards that my main worry is getting too high. So, I respond 1♡. If partner next bids 1♠, great; otherwise, I will let the spades go.

In fact, partner surprises me by raising to 2♡. Now that we've found a trump fit, my hand has playing potential. I might establish my second suit by ruffing in the dummy and my void in a suit North didn't bid is encouraging. I jump to 4♡. It's IMPs, where bringing home games is the goal; but I would make the same call at matchpoints.

All pass and West leads the ◇10.

Dlr: North
Vul: E-W

♠ A 6 3
♡ K 10 5
♢ J 2
♣ A 9 7 6 3

♠ J 8 7 4 2
♡ A J 9 8 3 2
♢ —
♣ 5 4

West	North	East	South
	1♣	pass	1♡
pass	2♡	pass	4♡
all pass			

I agree with North's raise to 2♡. Given that he had opened that hand — and with two-and-a-half quick tricks and a five-card suit, most players would — raising my major-suit response was best.

East plays the king on the first diamond and looks deflated when I ruff. To make this game, I must pick up the trumps; but there is no rush. I lead up to the ♠A and play another spade. East takes the king — West follows with the five and ten — and shifts to the ♣2: four, jack, ace. On the next spade, East discards a diamond and West takes the queen. He cashes the ♣K and leads another diamond; I ruff again.

I try to piece together the East hand. He started with ♠K9 and, apparently, ♣Q1082. He had some number of diamonds headed by the AK. But with at least 12 points and five decent diamonds (and 2-2-5-4 shape), many Easts would have climbed in with a 1♢ overcall, so I'm placing East with only four diamonds — and therefore three hearts.

I lead a trump to the king — both defenders play low — and return a trump. East follows low and I finesse. Maybe my reasoning was sound; West discards a diamond and we are +420. The full deal:

	North	
	♠ A 6 3	
	♡ K 10 5	
	◇ J 2	
	♣ A 9 7 6 3	
West		**East**
♠ Q 10 5		♠ K 9
♡ 4		♡ Q 7 6
◇ Q 10 9 6 5 4 3		◇ A K 8 7
♣ K J		♣ Q 10 8 2
	South	
	♠ J 8 7 4 2	
	♡ A J 9 8 3 2	
	◇ –	
	♣ 5 4	

At the other table, my teammate in East was a bidder. When North opened 1♣, East got his entry fee's worth by overcalling 1◇. I am no fan of four-card overcalls but my teammate's action gained here. South bid 1♡ but West leaped to 5◇. Nobody could act over that and East-West achieved a rare vulnerable-against-not paying sacrifice. North-South managed to take their three aces for +100 and we gained 7 IMPs.

59

In a Sectional Swiss Teams, my team has done well enough and is playing for all the cookies in the final match. Our opponents are capable players and occasional teammates. The first two boards are normal games, the third is a partscore deal on which we go plus. On the fourth deal, both sides are vulnerable and, as South, I hold:

♠ A J 2
♡ A 7 5 3 2
◇ 7 6
♣ K 4 2

My partner, the dealer, opens 1♣. I respond 1♡ and he raises to 2♡. Even if he were apt to open light, shapely hands, my hand would be worth game. Since I know his style — he embraces sound opening bids as I do — I can jump comfortably to 4♡. All pass, West leads the ♡Q and partner tables his dummy with a rueful comment as to the quality of his trump support.

Dlr: North
Vul: Both

♠ 6 3
♡ 8 6 4
◇ A K 4 2
♣ A Q 5 3

♠ A J 2
♡ A 7 5 3 2
◇ 7 6
♣ K 4 2

West	North	East	South
	1♣	pass	1♡
pass	2♡	pass	4♡
all pass			

North had a hard hand to describe. He would certainly rather have had four-card heart support or at least three strong hearts. If I had had a weak hand and four poor hearts, we might have reached a silly contract. But no other plan was appealing. Say he opens 1◇, as many players do with four cards in each minor, and rebids 2♣ over my 1♡ response. Then, if I bid 2◇

or 3♣ or 2NT next (or 3♢ if that bid were invitational), his hand wouldn't be strong enough to go on and he would never get to show his heart tolerance. Moreover, if I held:

♠ 8 7 5 2 ♡ A 7 5 3 2 ♢ Q 3 ♣ J 2

I would take a 2♢ preference and we would land in a 4-2 fit when we had a 5-3 heart fit.

Partner's alternative would be to rebid 1NT but his spade holding made that unattractive. (Incidentally, his raise to 2♡ was made without a pause that would have betrayed uncertainty; he had planned his second bid in the case where I responded 1♡.)

I have no problem with the auction and it's history now. I must see to winning ten tricks. Since I can only ruff one spade in dummy, I can afford to duck the opening lead. West continues with the ♡J, East follows low and I take the ace. East appears to have the ♡K, so I can cross to dummy and lead a spade to my jack, preparing to ruff my third spade in dummy. But it occurs to me that West is not trustworthy. He is good enough to have made a deceptive lead. Instead, I set out to reverse the dummy.

I take the ♢AK and ruff a diamond, lead a club to the queen and ruff the last diamond as East discards a spade. Next, I take the ♣K and lead a third club. West discards a spade and dummy's ace scores. Having won the previous eight tricks, I ruff dummy's last club. West overruffs with the king(!) but I win two more tricks with my ♠A and dummy's third trump.

West was out to get me. The full deal is:

	♠ 6 3 ♡ 8 6 4 ♢ A K 4 2 ♣ A Q 5 3	
♠ K 10 8 5 ♡ K Q J ♢ J 9 8 3 ♣ 10 8	N W E S	♠ Q 9 7 4 ♡ 10 9 ♢ Q 10 5 ♣ J 9 7 6
	♠ A J 2 ♡ A 7 5 3 2 ♢ 7 6 ♣ K 4 2	

If I try for a spade ruff in dummy, West will get in to cash his high trump, holding me to nine tricks.

At the other table, North embarked on the bidding plan my partner rejected. North opened 1♢ and rebid 2♣. South was handicapped not only because he didn't know about North's heart holding but also because North-South's style involved wide-ranging opening bids. So, South settled for a 2NT rebid and North could see no reason to move over that. After a spade opening lead, South managed nine tricks for +150.

Light opening bids have undeniable advantages but a sounder style is a better basis for accurate constructive bidding. As to the choice of which minor to open with North's hand, expert opinion is divided. Whether North's hand here was suitable for a raise to 2♡ is a matter for debate; but this time, his raise showed a gain.

60

A chicken-or-egg question of bridge theory is whether to open 1NT with, or despite, a five-card major suit; especially with five hearts. Some players believe in describing a hand's strength and approximate shape in a single bid; others would rather have a root canal than suppress a five-card major.

If you open 1♡ with:

♠Q4 ♡AJ953 ◇AK5 ♣Q73

what will you bid next if your partner responds 1♠? If you open 1NT instead, how will you like going minus when he passes with:

♠53 ♡Q1062 ◇876 ♣KJ94

and at least eight tricks are possible in hearts?

Some players would open 1NT with:

♠K6 ♡J9853 ◇AK5 ♣AJ5

because the hearts are ragged. But an advocate for opening 1♡ would argue that you may need time to set up that suit: time that may not be available in notrump.

One deal proves nothing and the debate will continue; but in the first match after the lunch break in a Sectional Swiss Teams, I am South with:

♠ AKQ1075
♡ K103
◇ 3
♣ 965

Both sides are vulnerable and East, the dealer, opens 1♡. I overcall 1♠, West passes and my partner cuebids 2♡. In our methods, he is showing a sound raise to 2♠ or better. A 2♠ raise would suggest a weaker hand; a jump to 3♠ would be preemptive.

East passes. I like my sixth spade and my ♡K appears to be positioned well. Many players would bid 4♠; but since simple overcalls are disciplined in our style, I settle for a jump to 3♠. North raises to 4♠, everyone passes and West leads the ♡J.

Dlr: East
Vul: Both

♠ J 8 2
♡ A 7 6
◇ J 9 6 5 4
♣ K 8

♠ A K Q 10 7 5
♡ K 10 3
◇ 3
♣ 9 6 5

West	North	East	South
		1♡	1♠
pass	2♡	pass	3♠
pass	4♠	all pass	

That's a fortunate lead: I can take dummy's ace and pick up the hearts. East, who opened the bidding, is sure to have the ♣A; but I can make the contract if I can ruff a club in dummy. Suppose I cross to my hand with a trump and lead a club to the king and ace. If East returns a heart, I win with the ten and cash another high trump. If the trumps break 2-2, I will be safe; if West started with three, I will go down one since he will get a heart ruff — or, if I draw trumps, I will lose two more clubs.

Suppose East has three trumps. Then he will lead a second trump when he takes the ♣A and a third trump when he wins a second club: down one again.

So, on the second trick, I lead the ♣8 from dummy. East wins with the queen, ponders and leads another heart; my ten wins. Now I have to guess. I cash the ♠A and West follows with the nine. If that's a subtle falsecard, well done to him. I concede a second club and when East leads a third heart, my king wins as West pitches a diamond. (Whew!) So, I ruff my last club in dummy, draw trumps and claim ten tricks for +620. The full deal:

♠ J 8 2
♡ A 7 6
◇ J 9 6 5 4
♣ K 8

West		East
♠ 9	N	♠ 6 4 3
♡ J 2	W E	♡ Q 9 8 5 4
◇ Q 10 8 7 2	S	◇ A K
♣ J 10 7 4 3		♣ A Q 2

♠ A K Q 10 7 5
♡ K 10 3
◇ 3
♣ 9 6 5

For what it's worth, at the other table, East opened 1NT and South overcalled 2♠. North raised and they got to game but West led the ♣J. Declarer was able to ruff his third club in dummy, but he still lost two clubs, a diamond and a heart; my team gained 12 IMPs.

I have no strong theoretical feelings about the best opening bid with hands similar to East's 3-5-2-3 hand. Like most players, I judge case by case, taking many factors into account.

61

Some deals in this book are constructed to illustrate a point of technique; but this is a deal I played one June at the Birmingham Duplicate Bridge Club. I was participating in 'The Longest Day' effort to benefit the Alzheimer's Association.

As South, the dealer, with both sides vulnerable, I hold:

♠ A 4
♡ K 10 9 6 2
◇ K 8 4
♣ A J 7

This is the old question I treated in the previous deal. Should I open 1♡ or 1NT? Some players (including the late Edgar Kaplan, a great theorist) absolutely refuse to suppress a five-card major; they remember the time they opened 1NT on:

♠J 4 2 ♡K Q 10 6 2 ◇A Q 8 ♣A 7

and played there opposite:

♠3 ♡A 9 8 5 ◇K 4 3 2 ♣6 5 4 3

Others stress the merits of conveying a hand's strength and approximate shape in a single bid. I have no strong feelings; but this time, I judge to open 1NT. I hold a 15-count with prime values and good intermediates in hearts. If I open 1♡ and hear a 1♠ response, a 1NT rebid will be an underbid.

Over my 1NT, my partner bids 2♡, a transfer. Uh-oh. My 1NT opening would have been more defensible if I had held three cards in spades. As it is, partner may be about to drop me in 2♠, stranding us in a 5-2 fit when we may have a 5-3 heart fit. But when I accept the transfer, partner continues with 2NT. I still like my hand but it's a minimum and I can't stretch to an iffy game at matchpoints. We may belong in hearts; but if I bid 3♡, I'm afraid that my partner may treat it as forcing.

West leads the ♣K and my fears are realized when I see dummy.

Dlr: South	♠ K 7 6 3 2
Vul: Both	♡ A Q 4
	◊ 5 3
	♣ 9 5 3
	♠ A 4
	♡ K 10 9 6 2
	◊ K 8 4
	♣ A J 7

West	North	East	South
			1NT
pass	2♡	pass	2♠
pass	2NT	all pass	

I let the ♣K win; but East has discouraged with the deuce and West shifts to the ♠J. I duck that in both hands and, when the jack holds, West continues with the ♠10 to my ace.

Assuming a decent heart break, I see eight tricks — nine if the ◊A is onside. But I think I have to hope that West has the ◊A; if East has it, we might be able to take ten tricks in hearts and some pairs may therefore even be +620 with our cards. Moreover, it occurs to me that if West didn't have the ◊A, he might have shifted to a diamond on the second or third trick.

I take the ♡AQ, East-West follow, and the ♠K. West discards a diamond. I cash three more hearts, West pitching a club and another diamond, and lead the ♣A and ♣J to West. As I hope, he can take his ◊A but has to give me the thirteenth trick with my ◊K. Making three. The full deal:

West	North / South	East
	♠ K 7 6 3 2	
	♡ A Q 4	
	◊ 5 3	
	♣ 9 5 3	
♠ J 10	N	♠ Q 9 8 5
♡ J 7 5	W E	♡ 8 3
◊ A 10 6 2	S	◊ Q J 9 7
♣ K Q 10 4		♣ 8 6 2
	♠ A 4	
	♡ K 10 9 6 2	
	◊ K 8 4	
	♣ A J 7	

Our +150 was a lucky result. At tables where South opened 1♡ and played in some number of hearts, no declarer won more than nine tricks.

62

My team has reached the final of a Sectional Knockout Teams. My partner is a good player with idiosyncrasies when it comes to bidding. Our opponents are a team capable of beating us and, indeed, are leading against us at halftime.

Midway through the second half, neither side is vulnerable and, as South, I hold:

♠ J 8 5 3
♡ A Q 10 9
◇ K J 9
♣ 9 5

West, the dealer, opens 1♡, my partner doubles and East jumps to 3♡, preemptive.

As I have mentioned, a bidding trend I dislike is the tendency to treat many low-level competitive doubles as 'card-showing' or 'action' on the theory that pursuing a penalty won't be worthwhile. The opponents can bid whatever they like with little fear of being doubled and clobbered. As much as I would love to hammer 3♡ for business, I can't do it. My partner would treat a double as 'responsive', showing some strength but lacking a good bid.

With this much strength, I need to do something. Frustration gets the better of me, and I unwisely bid 3♠, counting on partner for spade support. West passes, and my partner huddles... and bids 6♠! I bet that if I make this one, the match will be tied. West leads the ♣Q.

Dlr: West
Vul: None

North:
♠ A 10 9 6 4 2
♡ –
◇ A 8 7 6 2
♣ A K

South:
♠ J 8 5 3
♡ A Q 10 9
◇ K J 9
♣ 9 5

West	North	East	South
1♡	Dbl	3♡	3♠
pass	6♠	all pass	

North's double wouldn't have been everyone's choice but it could have worked well if my hand had been:

♠3 ♡J7632 ♢KJ943 ♣76

If he overcalls 1♠, as many players would, he might just play there when we could make 7♢.

I may have a diamond and a trump to lose in 6♠ but I can see a chance. I take the ♣A and cash the ♠A; East follows low, West with the queen. Next, I take the ♣K and exit with a trump; West wins in what I imagine is this position:

	♠ 10 9 6 4 ♡ – ♢ A 8 7 6 2 ♣ –	
♠ – ♡ K 8 7 6 2 ♢ Q 10 4 ♣ 10	N W E S	♠ – ♡ J 5 4 3 ♢ 5 3 ♣ 8 7 6
	♠ J 8 ♡ A Q 10 9 ♢ K J 9 ♣ –	

I believe I may make it. If West leads a diamond, I get a free finesse; if he leads a club, I ruff in dummy, discard a diamond from my hand and set up the diamonds with a ruff. If West leads a heart, I discard a diamond from dummy and if East plays the jack, I take the queen, discard another diamond from dummy on the ♡A and lead the ♡10 for a ruffing finesse against West's king and so a third diamond pitch.

If East withholds his ♡J or if West started with both the king and jack, I'm still safe. I take the ♡10 and ♡A, discarding diamonds from dummy, ruff a heart and run the trumps. West will be squeezed in the red suits.

But West has been thinking. After what seems a timeless interval, he comes forth with... the ♡K! The full deal:

	North	
	♠ A 10 9 6 4 2 ♡ — ♢ A 8 7 6 2 ♣ A K	
West		**East**
♠ K Q ♡ K 8 7 6 2 ♢ Q 10 4 ♣ Q J 10	N / W E / S	♠ 7 ♡ J 5 4 3 ♢ 5 3 ♣ 8 7 6 4 3 2
	South	
	♠ J 8 5 3 ♡ A Q 10 9 ♢ K J 9 ♣ 9 5	

I have no answer to that play. I can only discard two diamonds from dummy and must lose a diamond to West's queen. When somebody finds a world-class defensive play, all you can do is hand it to them.

In hindsight, I could, and perhaps should, have bid 3NT over East's 3♡. My partner would have converted to 4♠ and there we would have rested. Of course, my best action — if only the rules allowed it — would have been to take a few extra red cards from the bidding box to say, "I double for penalty." We would be +800.

Those 'do something intelligent, partner' doubles do bother me. Not only can they allow opponents to bid with impunity, they can also foster ethical problems. Experienced experts are careful to double in tempo or to avoid taking advantage of a double not made in tempo. But less-experienced players, who lack a mature sense of ethics, may let themselves be influenced, even if only subconsciously, by a slow double.

63

Bridge has diverse elements; that is part of its attraction. It embraces psychology as well as technique — those two elements can often conflict and the result is enigmatic.

In a local teams event, my partner, the dealer, with both sides vulnerable, opened 2NT with:

♠ A Q 8
♡ A K 4 3
◇ A K 6 3
♣ 4 2

I don't know that I would have done the same. I have a distaste for 2NT openings; they are space-consuming and may impede game or slam investigation. Opening 1◇ keeps the auction low and there are few hands with which partner will pass 1◇ but respond to 2NT. But his bid did lead to a prosaic auction: I raised to 3NT and everyone passed.

West led the ♠10 and my partner surveyed this:

Dlr: South
Vul: Both

♠ K 7 3
♡ 6 2
◇ 7 2
♣ Q J 10 6 5 3

♠ A Q 8
♡ A K 4 3
◇ A K 6 3
♣ 4 2

West	North	East	South
			2NT
pass	3NT	all pass	

He won with the ♠A, preserving dummy's king as an entry, and led a club: nine, ten, ace. East switched to the ◇10; South took the king and led another club: seven, jack... and East discarded a spade.

My partner was sunk. He couldn't use his clubs and the defenders discarded carefully and deprived him of a third trick in a red suit. Down one. The full deal:

	North	
	♠ K 7 3 ♡ 6 2 ◊ 7 2 ♣ Q J 10 6 5 3	
♠ 10 9 5 ♡ 10 7 5 ◊ J 5 4 ♣ K 9 8 7	N W E S	♠ J 6 4 2 ♡ Q J 9 8 ◊ Q 10 9 8 ♣ A
	♠ A Q 8 ♡ A K 4 3 ◊ A K 6 3 ♣ 4 2	

South's play was wrong in theory but the position was enigmatic. A defender who held Ax or Kx in clubs could duck the first club lead, and declarer would lack the entries to establish and cash the long clubs. South's technically correct play (which would win two overtricks as the cards lay) was to play low from dummy on the first club, hoping East had a singleton honor.

"What should I do?" my partner pleaded. "Play for the legitimate chance or hope a defender with honor-x makes a mistake and wins the first club? What if East's clubs are AK9? Then I lose an extra undertrick."

"It depends on your assessment of your opponent's skill," I shrugged. "I wouldn't like to insult my opponent by playing for a defensive error but inducing errors and taking advantage of them are a part of the game."

Incidentally, we lost 12 IMPs on the board. At the other table, the auction and opening lead were the same and so was the play to the first two tricks. But when East took the ♣A, he returned a spade, which altered the timing just enough to matter. Declarer won in his hand and led a second club to the jack again but when East discarded a spade, declarer cashed the ♠K and led a third club. On that trick, East had to discard a red card and South discarded from the other red suit and was able to set up a third trick in the suit that East had discarded. Making three!

64

In a Sectional Flighted Pairs, my partner is an expert; our opponents are Flight B. With neither side vulnerable, I'm South, the dealer, and pick up a balanced 21-count.

♠ A Q J
♡ A K Q 7 4
◊ Q J 8
♣ Q 2

A 2NT opening bid will describe this hand but I don't like it. I don't like suppressing the five-card major and I never like opening 2NT and having to start looking for a contract at the three-level. A few pairs use a 2NT opening as a conventional preemptive action and I can understand that. I can't understand why some players go out of their way to open 2NT with only 19 points. Maybe they think the call has preemptive value.

Still, this is a pairs event and the field will open 2NT. As far as I know, the field has never won an event; but I'll go along with it this time and hope to win some matchpoints in the play.

When I open 2NT, my partner huddles and raises to 6NT. My right-hand opponent passes; but only after a perceptible hitch. I'm afraid that I know what that means. I opened 2NT with four queens and a pair of jacks; I won't be surprised if slam is down off the top.

West leads the ♠10 and, when dummy appears, my apprehension is confirmed.

Dlr: South
Vul: None

♠ K 7 2
♡ J 6
◊ 9 7 5
♣ A K 7 5 4

♠ A Q J
♡ A K Q 7 4
◊ Q J 8
♣ Q 2

West	North	East	South
			2NT
pass	6NT	all pass	

I'm not down yet; just headed in that direction. If clubs break 3-3 and the hearts break no worse than 4-2, I have thirteen tricks. But if clubs are 4-2, which is more likely, I only have eleven winners, even if the hearts treat me well. Do I have any chance but to rely on a friendly club break?

I see two options. One is to assume that each defender has a high diamond, win the first spade in dummy and lead a diamond to my jack. If West wins and unsuspectingly leads another spade, I can run my major-suit winners, making the slam if clubs break 3-3 but also squeezing East in the minors if he had four clubs. I might try that play but the table action bothers me. East's hesitation suggests that he has the ♢AK. And if I'm wrong about the diamonds and I go down when clubs are 3-3 after all, I'll look silly.

Instead, I choose the other option: I run the hearts — they break 3-3 — and take my high spades, forcing East to discard in this position:

West	North	East
	♠ —	
	♡ —	
	♢ —	
	♣ A K 7 5 4	
♠ 8 4 3	N	♠ —
♡ —	W E	♡ —
♢ —	S	♢ A K
♣ J 8		♣ 10 9 6 3
	♠ —	
	♡ —	
	♢ Q J 8	
	♣ Q 2	

East can surrender his sword. If he throws a club, dummy's clubs will run. When he throws the ♢K, I force out his ♢A and win the rest. The full deal:

	North	
	♠ K 7 2 ♡ J 6 ♢ 9 7 5 ♣ A K 7 5 4	
♠ 10 9 8 4 3 ♡ 9 3 2 ♢ 6 3 2 ♣ J 8	N / W E / S	♠ 6 5 ♡ 10 8 5 ♢ A K 10 4 ♣ 10 9 6 3
	♠ A Q J ♡ A K Q 7 4 ♢ Q J 8 ♣ Q 2	

East was gracious enough to compliment my play instead of chewing on his partner for not leading a diamond. (A club lead would also have beaten 6NT.)

The next time you're in a hopeless contract — and we all reach such contracts — concede nothing. Recall the words of Winston Churchill: "Never give up. Never, ever give up."

65

I'm playing in a casual online team match. My partner is a friend of mine and an expert but he and I have no detailed systemic understandings. After a few uneventful deals, both sides are vulnerable and, as South, the dealer, I hold:

♠ A K 4 3
♡ K
◇ A 9 8 7 5
♣ A Q 5

I open 1◇ and my partner bids 1♡. My hand is potent enough to force to game after a response, so I jump shift to 2♠. (Though a non-jump change of suit by opener is not forcing, I know of pairs who treat a 1♠ rebid by opener as forcing. I won't risk my partner having a different view.)

The opponents continue to pass and partner raises to 4♠. What do I make of that?

For a long time, bidding was based on the idea that the better your hand, the more you bid. Then the 'minimum bidding' style and Two-over-One became prominent and the 'Principle of Fast Arrival' was an adjunct. Since jumps to game left no room for slam investigation, they discouraged further bidding.

West	**East**
1♡	2♣
2♠	4♠

Once West rebids 2♠ (and assuming that a reverse after East's two-level response suggests extra strength), East-West have the values for game. If you adhere to the classical approach, you expect East's jump to show good spade support and willingness to hear West bid more. With Fast Arrival, you expect only fair trump support and no slam aspirations. With a better hand, East would raise to 3♠.

I am no fan of Fast Arrival. Neither, apparently, are most experts, since 'Bridge World Standard', which is derived from an expert consensus, is a Slow Arrival system. After a Fast Arrival jump to game, you may have to guess whether to try for slam. Moreover, Fast Arrival has been known to arrive in the wrong contract.

I don't know my partner's opinion but, in any case, I think my hand is too promising to let go without a slam try; so, I bid 5♣.

Partner replies 5♡. I do know that he agrees with my feeling that a cue-bid shows slam interest. Partner would not feel compelled to show the ♡A if his hand didn't look reasonable for slam. My decision is still unclear, but all my values are slammish, so I bid 6♠. All pass and West leads the ♠10.

Dlr: South
Vul: Both

♠ Q J 7 6
♡ A 8 6 5 4 2
◇ 2
♣ J 6

♠ A K 4 3
♡ K
◇ A 9 8 7 5
♣ A Q 5

West	North	East	South
			1◇
pass	1♡	pass	2♠
pass	4♠	pass	5♣
pass	5♡	pass	6♠
all pass			

To make this, I will have to set up the hearts. I win the first trump with the ace, unblock the ♡K and consider. Suppose I lead a trump to dummy and East-West follow. I ruff a heart high, draw the remaining trump and take the ♡A. If the suit breaks 3-3, I am home. If it breaks 4-2, I concede a heart and succeed if the club finesse wins.

That line is not a certainty. Can I do better? What I need is an additional dummy entry to set up and cash the hearts even in the event of a 4-2 break. The only possible entry is the ♣J, so on the third trick, I lead the ♣Q.

West takes the king and leads another trump; I win in dummy. East follows. I ruff a heart, cross to the ♣J and ruff a heart. Then I can take the ◇A, ruff a diamond, draw the remaining trump and win the rest with master hearts. The first line of play I considered would have failed since the full deal is:

	North	
	♠ Q J 7 6 ♡ A 8 6 5 4 2 ♢ 2 ♣ J 6	
West ♠ 10 9 5 ♡ 10 9 ♢ K J 10 6 3 ♣ K 10 8	N W E S	**East** ♠ 8 2 ♡ Q J 7 3 ♢ Q 4 ♣ 9 7 4 3 2
	♠ A K 4 3 ♡ K ♢ A 9 8 7 5 ♣ A Q 5	

At the other table, South opened 2NT. Notrump openings with singleton honors seem to be all the rage but such an action here would not have crossed my mind. I never go out of my way to open 2NT (discussed in the previous two deals). North responded 3♣ and when South bid 3♠, North settled for a raise to 4♠. They were +650 and we gained 13 IMPs.

Over 3♠, I expect North might have tried 5♢ as a 'splinter bid' next. If South had interpreted that call correctly, he would surely have bid 6♠.

66

Choosing from more than one possible trump suit can be a taxing problem even for a world-class pair. A 4-4 fit may provide a vital extra trick or two by ruffing in either hand. A 5-3 fit may be safer if a good source of tricks is available elsewhere. A 6-2 fit may be best if declarer must keep control against a forcing defense. Even a 4-3 fit may offer the only chance.

In a local Swiss Teams, both sides are vulnerable and, as South, in third position, I hold:

♠ Q 10 7 4 2
♡ K Q 9 6 4
◊ A Q
♣ 6

After two passes, I open 1♠, the higher-ranking of my two long suits. It doesn't matter that the quality of my heart suit is stronger. West passes and my partner offers a limit raise to 3♠.

I suppose we might belong in hearts. My partner might have only three-card spade support; as a passed hand, he would be nervous about a temporizing response in a new suit because I might drop him there. But I can't afford to try 4♡ because North would doubtless treat it as a try for slam, not as an offer to play. So I just bid 4♠ and everyone passes. Concealing my second suit from the defenders may be beneficial anyway.

West leads the ♡2.

Dlr: North
Vul: Both

♠ J 9 8 5
♡ A J 10 5
◊ K 10 3
♣ Q 4

♠ Q 10 7 4 2
♡ K Q 9 6 4
◊ A Q
♣ 6

West	North	East	South
	pass	pass	1♠
pass	3♠	pass	4♠
all pass			

That lead looks, waddles and quacks like a singleton, so I'm in danger of four losers. If I win and lead a trump, West may win, lead a club to East and ruff a heart return and I'll still have a high trump to lose.

I may not be able to do anything about that but I can lose nothing by trying. I take the ♡J, come to the ◇A, overtake the ◇Q with dummy's king and continue with the ◇10. When East follows low, I discard my club loser. As it happens, I get lucky because the full deal is:

West		East
	♠ J 9 8 5 ♡ A J 10 5 ◇ K 10 3 ♣ Q 4	
♠ A 6 ♡ 2 ◇ J 9 6 4 ♣ J 10 8 7 3 2	N W E S	♠ K 3 ♡ 8 7 3 ◇ 8 7 5 2 ♣ A K 9 5
	♠ Q 10 7 4 2 ♡ K Q 9 6 4 ◇ A Q ♣ 6	

West takes the ◇J but East's club entry is no more. As the trumps lie, West has no way to score his low trump and I lose only to the king and ace, making four.

This time, hearts would have been the better trump suit. If West had held a singleton spade and led it to get a ruff and beat 4♡, that would have been a misfortune.

I didn't care for my partner's 3♠ bid. My idea of a limit raise is a hand with primary values and distribution. I would raise a 1♠ opening to 3♠ with:

♠ K 5 4 3 ♡ A J 7 5 ◇ 3 ♣ 10 7 6 4

Had partner not been a passed hand, I might even have understood an exceedingly old-fashioned response of 2♡. As it was, he had little choice but to raise spades directly. (Many pairs would have used Drury, a conventional, fit-showing 2♣ response by a passed hand. That wasn't part of our methods but partner could have jump-shifted to 3♡ — fit-showing by a passed hand.)

At the other table, North-South believed in opening light and North started with 1♢, South responded 1♠ and North raised to 2♠. Then South, an optimist as well as a light opener, visualized a slam if North held a hand such as:

♠ A J 9 3 ♡ A 3 ♢ J 6 5 3 ♣ A 7 5

The old wisdom is never to play your partner for perfect cards — he won't have them — but South tried 3♡ and North, perhaps thinking that the search for the best trump suit was still on and that a 4-4 heart fit might produce a trick more than spades, lifted to 4♡. South, not on the same page (nor even in the same library), thought his partner had made an encouraging noise with a far better hand. He cuebid 5♢ and the resulting five-level contract was unmakeable.

67

In a Sectional Swiss Teams, only our side is vulnerable and as South, the dealer, I hold a promising hand.

♠ A K J 7 6
♡ Q 6 4 3
♢ A K Q 7
♣ –

My hand actually holds more promise than our system can live up to. I must open 1♠ and, if my partner declines to respond with a hand such as:

♠ 4 3 ♡ K J 9 5 2 ♢ 8 3 ♣ 8 7 5 3

we will be marooned at 1♠ when we might make 6♡. No system is foolproof, nor is any system better than the players using it, but a weakness in both Standard and Two-over-One is the wide range for an opening one-bid. Strong Club systems have an edge in that area and shortcomings in others.

As it happens, West passes, my partner raises to 2♠ and East comes in with 3♣. Since the right minimum for North —

♠ Q 5 4 3 ♡ A 5 ♢ J 5 4 ♣ 8 6 5 3

— will provide good play for 6♠, I must try to get there. To start, I cuebid 4♣ to suggest a club control and slam interest. West boosts to 5♣ and two passes follow.

We may still have a slam and I doubt we can mangle 5♣, especially when North couldn't double it. So I continue with a 5♢ cuebid and when my partner comes back with 5♡, I must decide whether to take the plunge.

Some experts would feel obliged to bid 5♡ — a 'free' cuebid — with any old hand containing the ♡A. My philosophy — and I suspect I'm in the minority — is that a cuebid shows slam interest. Unless North were willing to encourage slam, he would sign off in 5♠ whether he had the ♡A or not. Granted, he didn't cuebid 5♡ directly over 5♣, so he might feel obliged to cuebid now.

I think this is my gamble to take, so I jump to 6♠. all pass; West leads the ♣3.

Dlr: South
Vul: N-S

	♠ Q 10 5 4 3
	♡ A 7 5 2
	◇ 10 3
	♣ J 6
	♠ A K J 7 6
	♡ Q 6 4 3
	◇ A K Q 7
	♣ –

West	North	East	South
			1♠
pass	2♠	3♣	4♣
5♣	pass	pass	5◇
pass	5♡	pass	6♠
all pass			

That's as good a dummy as I could hope for. North might have jumped to 6♠ over my 5◇. Still, I haven't yet won twelve tricks. East plays the ♣K; I ruff and draw trumps, finding East with two. Next, I take my three top diamonds, pitching a heart from dummy, and ruff my last diamond. West discards a club; East's diamonds were J962. Then, I ruff dummy's last club.

East may well hold the ♡K for his three-level entry into the auction but that is no certainty. I do have a count of the distribution: West's lead of the ♣3 marks him with at most five clubs, so East had at least six. East also had two trumps and four diamonds, hence one heart at most.

So I have a sure thing: I lead the ♡3 and, when West follows with the eight, play low from dummy. East wins with the nine and is endplayed. He must concede a ruff-and-sluff, and I ruff with the last trump in my hand and discard dummy's last low heart.

If West had played the ten on the first heart, I would have ducked in dummy, forcing him to lead away from his ♡K or concede a ruff-and-sluff. We are +1430. The full deal is:

	North	
	♠ Q 10 5 4 3 ♡ A 7 5 2 ♢ 10 3 ♣ J 6	
West ♠ 8 ♡ K J 10 8 ♢ 8 5 4 ♣ Q 9 5 3 2	N W E S	**East** ♠ 9 2 ♡ 9 ♢ J 9 6 2 ♣ A K 10 8 7 4
	♠ A K J 7 6 ♡ Q 6 4 3 ♢ A K Q 7 ♣ —	

The same endplay would have worked if East's shape had been 2=0=4=7 (though then he might have doubled 6♠ to suggest a non-club opening lead). If East had shown out on my third high diamond — and I had judged to play him for 2=3=2=6 shape — I could have ruffed the fourth diamond and continued with the ♡A and a heart to my queen and, if West won with the doubleton king, he would be endplayed.

What if East had been 2=2=3=6 or 2=2=2=7? Then the slam could still be made no matter who held the ♡K but I would have to guess who had it.

At the other table, North-South reached 6♠ but my teammates didn't believe that saves are only for the Red Cross. They judged to sacrifice in 7♣ doubled, minus 1100, and we gained 8 IMPs.

68

In a Sectional Open Pairs, I have an advancing partner. Both sides are vulnerable, and I am North with a balanced 12-count:

♠ A J 8 7
♡ Q 4
◇ A 10 4
♣ J 10 9 5

My partner, the dealer, opens 1♠; West passes. This hand is a complete high-card minimum for forcing; but I do have two tens and to stay out of game in a one-session pairs game is to invite a zero. So I respond 2NT, the forcing raise in our methods. I actually prefer to use a different bid as a forcing raise; the old-style natural and forcing 2NT response, showing a balanced hand with side-suit stoppers, can be too valuable to give up, in my opinion.

The opponents stay out and my partner ponders and bids 3♠, a suggestion for slam. If he were content to play in 4♠, he would have bid it.

I suppose I could cuebid 4◇ now; some experts would. Since my hand is a dead minimum, I prefer to sign off in 4♠; but South persists with 5♣. Now I can cuebid 5◇ and he tries 5♡. He may be trying to get to a grand slam but I can only bid 5♠. Partner carries on to 6♠, passed out.

West leads the ♡J and partner has this to work with:

Dlr: South
Vul: Both

♠ A J 8 7
♡ Q 4
◊ A 10 4
♣ J 10 9 5

♠ K Q 10 9 5 3 2
♡ A 5
◊ K J 3
♣ A

West	North	East	South
			1♠
pass	2NT	pass	3♠
pass	4♠	pass	5♣
pass	5◊	pass	5♡
pass	5♠	pass	6♠
all pass			

He plays dummy's ♡Q but East covers with the king. Declarer takes the ace and cogitates. He cashes the ♣A, leads a trump to dummy and returns the ♣J, pitching his losing heart when East follows low. West takes the queen and leads a high heart.

My partner ruffs that and takes the ◊KA. When no queen appears, he leads dummy's ♣10. When East plays low, South throws his ◊J… but West produces the ♣K for down one. The full deal:

North:
♠ A J 8 7
♡ Q 4
◊ A 10 4
♣ J 10 9 5

West:
♠ 6
♡ J 10 9 8
◊ 8 6 5 2
♣ K Q 6 3

East:
♠ 4
♡ K 7 6 3 2
◊ Q 9 7
♣ 8 7 4 2

South:
♠ K Q 10 9 5 3 2
♡ A 5
◊ K J 3
♣ A

"The double ruffing finesse looked like a sure thing," my partner says ruefully. "I thought the man would have led the ♣K if he had had both honors."

I could afford to be supportive of my partner's effort. He had bid his hand well and made a disciplined stop in 6♠. He drew a reasonable, though unproductive, inference from the opening lead and gave himself an extra chance for the slam by cashing the top diamonds. But the late chess master Bobby Fischer offered this advice: "You have found a good move. Bravo! But wait. There may be a better move."

South should lead a trump to dummy at the third trick, ruff a club and cross to dummy in trumps to ruff two more clubs. Then he exits with a heart. When West wins, he must lead either another heart, conceding a fatal ruff-and-sluff, or a diamond, guessing the queen for declarer.

69

In a Sectional Swiss Teams, I have a partner who is as bold in the bidding as I am conservative. Sometimes, a partnership of opposing styles works surprisingly well; the players allow for each other's approaches and the result is a successful balance.

Both sides are vulnerable and, as South, the dealer, I hold:

♠ K 10 9 8 3
♡ A
◇ A Q
♣ 8 6 5 4 3

I open 1♠ — I discuss my preference for opening the major in the following deal — and we have the auction to ourselves. My partner responds 2NT, an artificial forcing spade raise. Since he didn't issue a 'splinter' response or take the opportunity to show a strong side suit, he will invariably have balanced distribution. I bid 3♡, conventionally showing a singleton heart. (I would rather not have the singleton ace.) Partner cuebids 4♣; I reply with a 4◇ cuebid. He bids 4♠.

I suppose I could try again with 5♡. In our style, partner's 4♣ showed slam interest. He would not feel obliged to issue a cuebid — even a 'free' cuebid below game — with a hand that didn't look slammish. In many partnerships, North would be obliged to cuebid 4♣ no matter what the rest of his hand looked like. Remember my view: that that style dilutes a major advantage of cuebidding controls, which is to let either partner use judgment.

My general approach to slam bidding is, 'If we may have a slam, make a try. Involve your partner.' Still, I'm not sure we would be safe at the five-level. North would have cuebid 4♣ with:

♠ A J 7 2 ♡ Q 5 4 ◇ K 3 2 ♣ A 10 7

and, knowing him, he might have bid 5◇ over my 4◇. After thinking it over, I pass.

West leads the ♣Q and dummy is downright depressing.

Dlr: South Vul: Both	♠ A Q 7 2 ♡ J 7 3 ◊ 7 3 ♣ A K 7 2
	♠ K 10 9 8 3 ♡ A ◊ A Q ♣ 8 6 5 4 3

West	North	East	South
			1♠
pass	2NT	pass	3♡
pass	4♣	pass	4◊
pass	4♠(!)	all pass	

My partner picked the wrong time to abandon his aggressive style. With good trumps and little wasted heart strength opposite my singleton, he was worth a second cuebid of 5♣ over my 4◊. Then I am sure I would have bid 6♠. If clubs are 2-2, we have missed a grand slam.

When you've had a bidding debacle, it's not easy to put it behind you and concentrate on the play. I try to force myself to stay focused. If I play a club honor from dummy and East follows, I will take twelve or thirteen tricks. But what if West has led from QJ109? A 4-0 break is against the odds but possible. If East ruffs dummy's ♣A and shifts to a diamond, I will be in bad shape in 4♠. If the finesse loses, West will lead another club, East will ruff dummy's second honor and West will get two clubs for down two.

I may look silly; but to safeguard the contract, I play low from dummy on the first club — and East discards! When West leads another club, dummy plays low again. East ruffs the third club and leads a diamond but I can take the ace, draw trumps, cash the ♣A and discard dummy's last diamond on my fifth club. Making four (whew!) for +620. The full deal:

	North	
	♠ A Q 7 2 ♡ J 7 3 ◇ 7 3 ♣ A K 7 2	
West		**East**
♠ J ♡ Q 9 8 4 ◇ K 10 6 2 ♣ Q J 10 9	N W E S	♠ 6 5 4 ♡ K 10 6 5 2 ◇ J 9 8 5 4 ♣ —
	South	
	♠ K 10 9 8 3 ♡ A ◇ A Q ♣ 8 6 5 4 3	

At the other table, South opened 1♣, North responded 1♠ and South raised to 3♠. North quite reasonably thought he was worth a try for slam; he cuebid 4♣. Since South had minimum high-card values for his jump-raise, he signed off in 4♠ and North respected the signoff, though he might have tried again by bidding 5♣.

East led a diamond and declarer carelessly finessed with dummy's queen. He swiftly found out what a bad idea that was. West won and shifted to the ♣Q; East ruffed declarer's ace. West eventually got two club tricks for down one and we gained 12 IMPs. Whether they were deserved, I cannot say.

70

Once upon a time, experts opened 1♣ on most hands with five spades and five clubs. They reasoned that partner was likely to respond in a red suit and then opener had an economical 1♠ rebid available. When I was a *Bulletin* editor more than thirty years ago, I recall writing an article suggesting that opening 1♠ was better. The magazine got so many letters from 1♣ bidders, including some world-class players, that I wound up soliciting an article from Edgar Kaplan, a 1♠ opener, to support my point of view.

I believe that most experts now open 1♠, except on extreme hands. The 1♠ opening gets the major suit mentioned quickly, lest it be lost, avoids some rebid problems and makes it harder for the opponents to come in. Moreover, if you open 1♣ and then bid spades twice, your partner may think you have six clubs and five spades.

In a Sectional Flighted Pairs, both sides are vulnerable and, as South, I hold:

♠ A K 8 7 4
♡ 6
◊ 8 3
♣ A K Q 5 2

East, the dealer, passes, I open 1♠ and my partner raises to 2♠. Maybe I should try for slam. Twelve tricks will be all but cold if he has a perfect minimum such as:

♠Q 9 5 2 ♡8 7 5 ◊A 5 2 ♣J 9 7

I could jump to 4♣ to show a two-suiter with slam interest; he would cue-bid 4◊ and we might reach 6♠. (Some pairs would treat a jump to 4♣ as shortness-showing.)

Still, partners rarely have exactly the right cards and if we end up stopping in game, I will have shown my second suit to the defenders. At matchpoints, I won't worry about missing an unlikely slam; if twelve tricks depend on receiving a friendly opening lead, I might get a good result just for being +680. So I jump to 4♠ and everyone passes. West huddles and leads the ♡A.

Dlr: South
Vul: Both

♠ J 10 9
♡ K 10 3 2
◊ Q J 6
♣ J 10 7

♠ A K 8 7 4
♡ 6
◊ 8 3
♣ A K Q 5 2

West	North	East	South
		pass	1♠
pass	2♠	pass	4♠
all pass			

I was worried about missing a slam, yet it will be no cinch to make game. But East signals with the ♡8 and when West leads another heart, I gratefully pitch a diamond on the ♡K. Now, I'm ahead of other declarers in 4♠ but am still unwilling to forgo the percentage play in trumps. Taking a slight risk, I take my ♠A, lead a club to dummy and let the ♠J ride. West takes the queen and leads another heart, so I ruff, draw the missing trump and claim +620, losing one diamond. The full deal:

North:
♠ J 10 9
♡ K 10 3 2
◊ Q J 6
♣ J 10 7

West:
♠ Q 5 2
♡ A 9 7 4
◊ K 10 5
♣ 8 4 3

East:
♠ 6 3
♡ Q J 8 5
◊ A 9 7 4 2
♣ 9 6

South:
♠ A K 8 7 4
♡ 6
◊ 8 3
♣ A K Q 5 2

West reproaches himself for not finding a diamond shift on the second trick; perhaps East should have signaled with a low heart on Trick 1.

Opening 1♠ with 5-5 in the blacks may have the benefit of letting you conceal your second suit. At some tables in my section, South opened 1♣ and the auction was 1♣-1♡; 1♠-1NT; 3♠-4♠. At one table, where the auction started 1♠-2♠, South jumped to 4♣ next and North signed off in 4♠. In those cases, West often led a diamond. If instead he led the ♡A, he shifted to diamonds, which couldn't cost. If South held Ax, he could pitch his low diamond on the ♡K anyway.

71

Matchpoint events are tests of skill but random factors can intrude — such as which boards you play against which opponents. If you are up against the top seed in your section for two boards, you should be happy to play 3NT on the first board with nine tricks, no more no less, and to defend a prosaic 4♠ on the second with a result of -420 that is as flat as a pancake.

Reality is different. A friend of mine swears that if he sits North-South and there is a slam for East-West that requires inspired lunacy to bid and crystal-ball play to make, he will be opposed by the only pair in the room capable of doing just that.

This is a deal in which I was a victim of fate. The setting was a Regional pairs event. Both sides were vulnerable and I was West, the dealer, with:

♠ J 6
♡ K 10 9
◇ 10 6 5
♣ Q 10 9 6 2

I passed, and North opened 1NT. East passed and South huddled and bid 6◇. After I passed, North started to think and after a timeless interval... he came forth with 7◇. Everyone passed, South with a sigh as heavy as a storm cloud.

I led the ♣10 and South was faced with finding thirteen tricks.

Dlr: West
Vul: Both

North:
♠ A K 9 5
♡ A J 7 6
◇ 7 4
♣ A 7 3

South:
♠ 10 7 4
♡ 5
◇ A K Q J 9 8 3 2
♣ 4

West	North	East	South
	1NT	pass	6◇
pass	7◇(!)	all pass	

I could understand North's bid; his wealth of prime values was seductive. Still, to pass or perhaps try 6NT would have been disciplined. North couldn't be sure of thirteen tricks.

South had play for the grand slam. He could double-finesse in spades, winning three tricks there if I had the Q-J, and there were remote squeeze chances. South took the ♣A and drew trumps; East threw a heart and two clubs. Then, South no longer liked his chances of finding me with both missing spade honors — East, void in trumps, probably had spade length — but my partner's heart discard brought hope.

South took three more trumps, pitching two spades from dummy to reach:

♠ A K
♡ A J 7 6
♢ –
♣ –

♠ 10 7 4
♡ 5
♢ 3 2
♣ –

East, who had started with:

♠ Q 8 3 2 ♡ Q 8 4 3 2 ♢ – ♣ K J 8 5

could turn in his sword. If he had saved two spades and four hearts, declarer could have taken the ♠AK and scored his ♠10 at the end. When East actually kept three spades and three hearts, declarer took the ♡A, ruffed a heart, led a spade to dummy, ruffed a heart and won the last two tricks with a high spade and a good heart.

"Lead a spade," my partner remarked to me.

"Doesn't matter," I shrugged. "Then the ♣A is an entry and the trump squeeze still operates."

In fact, no lead would beat the grand slam. We would have received a few matchpoints for -1440 against 6NT. You can guess how many we got for -2140. The full deal:

♠ A K 9 5
♡ A J 7 6
◇ 7 4
♣ A 7 3

♠ J 6	N	♠ Q 8 3 2
♡ K 10 9	W E	♡ Q 8 4 3 2
◇ 10 6 5	S	◇ —
♣ Q 10 9 6 2		♣ K J 8 5

♠ 10 7 4
♡ 5
◇ A K Q J 9 8 3 2
♣ 4

The modern expert approach is to 'bash into games, investigate for slams'. It's easy to understand why. Going down in a slam is painful: a game bonus is lost and the psychological effect on the partnership can be damaging. Still, I believe that experts are too cautious. 'Blasting' into a slam — bidding what you think you can make and daring the defenders to beat it — still has its place.

South must have felt that way. He thought he would have the material for twelve tricks in diamonds unless we took two first. South didn't bother to bid 4♣, Gerber, to ask for aces because, so he said, if North responded 4♠ to show two, East would have a chance to make a lead-directing double (or a lead-discouraging pass). If North held:

♠ A Q 6 3 ♡ A K 9 4 ◇ 10 4 ♣ K 6 3

South didn't want to deal with a spade on the opening lead.

As for the play, declarers often underestimate the power of cashing out a long suit and forcing the defenders to find discards. Having analyzed thousands of deals with Deep Finesse, I am continually amazed by what miracles can occur when declarer runs a suit. Even if a defender is not truly squeezed, he may face a tough guess.

Getting 'fixed' by being in the wrong place at the wrong time is a part of the game. In theory, luck should even out; but I've yet to meet the gremlins who are charged with enforcing that rule.

72

In a one-session club matchpoint game, both sides are vulnerable. My partner and I are a casual partnership and are using simple methods. As South, the dealer, I hold:

♠ A K Q 10 7 6
♡ A
◇ A Q
♣ 10 8 3 2

I wouldn't look down on opening 2♣. I can reasonably expect at least nine winners — six in spades, two red aces and either the ◇Q or a club trick — and I have four-and-a-half defensive tricks, which is adequate for a forcing opening. But because my partner won't imagine that I have four possible club losers after a 2♣ opening, I start with 1♠. I hope I won't play there when he fails to respond with a hand such as:

♠J 5 4 ♡9 8 7 6 5 ◇K 4 2 ♣5 4

Instead, North responds 2♡. I jump to 3♠, forcing, and he raises to 4♠.

Slam, maybe even a grand slam, is possible. North might hold:

♠J 9 8 ♡K Q J 6 5 ◇7 6 5 ♣A 6

though with that hand, some players might make an 'advance cuebid' of 4♣ over 3♠. I can cuebid 5◇ now but if North holds:

♠J 9 ♡K Q J 6 5 ◇K 7 6 ♣Q 7 6

we might go down at the five-level on the club lead I would then have invited.

I think I will just bid slam and let the defenders try to beat it. As I observed in the previous deal, the modern approach is 'blast into games, investigate for slams.' Experts tend toward caution in slam bidding because a losing slam costs a game bonus. But 'blasting' still has its place. If you know the values for slam are present, bid it straightaway and give the opening leader no guidance.

In a teams event, where I would have teammates to account to, I might be more discreet. But in a one-session pairs game, I can afford to be carefree, so I indulge myself with a jump to 6♠. Everyone passes and West mulls and leads a trump.

Dlr: South
Vul: Both

♠ J 9 8
♡ K J 8 5 4
◇ K J 10
♣ Q 5

♠ A K Q 10 7 6
♡ A
◇ A Q
♣ 10 8 3 2

West	North	East	South
			1♠
pass	2♡	pass	3♠
pass	4♠	pass	6♠
all pass			

It looks as though my gamble has paid off. I can count eleven tricks and have prospects for a twelfth trick with the hearts. When I play dummy's ♠8, East discards a diamond. I unblock my ♡A, lead a trump to dummy, ruff a heart, cross back to dummy with a trump and ruff a heart. East has discarded two more diamonds on the trumps and on the third heart, alas, West discards a diamond.

Well, so much for setting up the fifth heart. I think I'm going down but I can go down fighting. I cash my last trump, throwing the ♣5 from dummy, and take three diamonds. The ending is:

North:
♠ —
♡ K J
◇ —
♣ Q

West:
♠ —
♡ —
◇ —
♣ K 9 7

East:
♠ —
♡ Q 10
◇ —
♣ A J

South:
♠ —
♡ —
◇ —
♣ 10 8 3

East still has to find a discard and can't cope. If he discards the ♣J, I can exit with a club to endplay him. If he discards the ♣A to avoid the endplay, I lead the ♣Q. Then, if West ducks, I cash the ♡K; but if he takes the ♣K, he has to return a club from his 97 to my 108. Making six! The full deal:

	♠ J 9 8 ♡ K J 8 5 4 ♢ K J 10 ♣ Q 5	
♠ 5 4 3 2 ♡ 7 2 ♢ 8 5 3 ♣ K 9 7 4	N W E S	♠ – ♡ Q 10 9 6 3 ♢ 9 7 6 4 2 ♣ A J 6
	♠ A K Q 10 7 6 ♡ A ♢ A Q ♣ 10 8 3 2	

After our auction, with North showing a heart suit that might have provided me with discards, West might have done better to make an aggressive club lead.

I was wrong to bid 6♠. Our +1430 scored a top but nobody else got to slam or won twelve tricks; we would have gotten the same top for +680. So I risked a bottom for nothing.

As to the play... the lesson is never to give up on a contract. Odd things can happen when you cash out winners and force the defenders to discard.

73

In a Compact Knockout Teams at a Sectional, my team has survived its opening match and is pitted against a strong team next. The first few boards appear to be flat and then, as South, the dealer, I hold:

♠ A Q 10 6
♡ 6 2
◇ 7 4 3
♣ A K 6 3

Both sides are vulnerable. I open 1♣ and my partner responds 2♡. I can see a case for playing weak jump shifts at matchpoints (though even then, I fear that many pairs use them because they are fashionable — 'everybody plays them' — and not because those pairs have studied the results they achieve). At IMPs, where accurate game and slam bidding is a vital component, I prefer the strong treatment.

I bid 2♠ and my partner bids 2NT. Since I have little or nothing extra, all I can do is raise to 3NT. But then North tries 4♠ and I have to reconsider.

My partner appears to have good three-card spade support and a hand that looks attractive for slam. My spades are stout — the ♠10 may be a crucial card. I have prime values in clubs and may be able to ruff a club or two in dummy. Given my previous bidding, my hand can't be any better, so I bid 6♠, knowing I must cope with a 4-3 fit.

Everyone passes and West leads the ♣J.

Dlr: South	♠ K J 4
Vul: Both	♡ A K Q 8 4
	◇ A 5 2
	♣ 7 4
	♠ A Q 10 6
	♡ 6 2
	◇ 7 4 3
	♣ A K 6 3

West	North	East	South
			1♣
pass	2♡	pass	2♠
pass	2NT	pass	3NT
pass	4♠	pass	6♠
all pass			

This looks good, barring hideous breaks. I can count eleven tricks: four trumps, two clubs, one club ruff in dummy (I lack the entries to ruff two clubs comfortably), three high hearts and the ◊A. Suppose I take the ♣AK, ruff a club high and draw trumps, discarding dummy's low diamonds if trumps break 4-2. Then I will have none left but I can continue with the three top hearts. If that suit breaks 4-2, I can concede the fourth heart and will be safe unless the defender who wins happens to have a club to cash. If the trumps break 3-3, I can handle a 4-2 heart break.

That line looks reasonable — maybe it is best — but I see an alternative: I can duck a heart on the second trick and can expect to get home with normal breaks. I can't calculate the exact percentages in my head but my instinct, for what it's worth, suggests that the second line is superior. So I take the ♣A and play a low heart from both hands.

West wins with the nine, ponders and leads a trump. I win with dummy's jack, come to the ♣K and ruff a club with the ♠K. Then I draw trumps — they break 4-2 — and lead a heart to dummy. Both defenders follow, so I run the hearts and end with twelve tricks. The first line I considered would have failed since the full deal is:

West	North	East
	♠ K J 4 ♡ A K Q 8 4 ◊ A 5 2 ♣ 7 4	
♠ 9 5 3 2 ♡ 10 9 ◊ K 10 9 8 ♣ J 10 9	N W E S	♠ 8 7 ♡ J 7 5 3 ◊ Q J 6 ♣ Q 8 5 2
	♠ A Q 10 6 ♡ 6 2 ◊ 7 4 3 ♣ A K 6 3	

"I should have led a diamond," West says regretfully.

At the other table, where North-South were using weak jump shifts, the auction started 1♣-1♡; 1♠-2◇. South thought — and I would agree — that he could bid 2NT next despite his lack of a diamond stopper. North might have tried 3♡, forcing, or a quantitative 4NT next; but he was discouraged and merely raised to 3NT for +630. Slam never entered the picture.

We got to a decent contract and gained 13 IMPs but our luck was in. A diamond opening lead would not beat 6♠. I could duck, win the second diamond, take the ♣AK, ruff a club in dummy and draw trumps. The last trump would squeeze East in hearts and clubs. But a trump opening lead, which West might have found after our auction, would upset the timing for any successful line of play.

74

In a local Swiss Teams, I have a learning but promising partner. Only our side is vulnerable and, as South, I hold:

♠ K 6 3
♡ Q
◇ K Q 8 6 4 2
♣ 4 3 2

West, the dealer, opens 1♠. My partner doubles, East passes and I must choose an action. It's possible that we have no game — North could hold:

♠ 8 ♡ K J 6 5 ◇ A J 9 ♣ K Q 7 6 5

— but I have too much trick-taking power to let this hand go without at least inviting. I can jump to 2NT, invitational, or bash into 3NT. I can bid 3◇, invitational; 5◇ will be a favorite if North holds:

♠ 4 ♡ A K 7 6 ◇ 10 9 7 5 ♣ A Q 6 5

I think I should try 3◇; we will still have a chance to get to notrump. The opponents pass and North jumps to 5◇, passed out. West ponders and leads a trump.

Dlr: West
Vul: N-S

North:
♠ 7 4
♡ A 5 3
◇ A J 10
♣ A K 7 6 5

South:
♠ K 6 3
♡ Q
◇ K Q 8 6 4 2
♣ 4 3 2

West	North	East	South
1♠	dbl	pass	3◇
pass	5◇	all pass	

This is the wrong contract, alas. We have nine top tricks in notrump — 10 with a likely spade lead — and 5♦ is uncertain. I guess I could have bid notrump; but North could have bid 3♠ over 3♦, giving me a chance to try 3NT with a spade stopper.

I see eleven tricks: six diamonds, the ♥A and four clubs with a normal 3-2 break. But I have to concede a club to establish the suit and if East wins a club trick, he will lead a deadly spade through my king.

What I need to do is lose a club to West. Suppose he has Qx. I can win the opening lead in my hand, lead a club to the ace, get back with a trump and lead a second club, ducking West's queen. But that approach will fail if East has Qxx (or if West has ♣Qx and a singleton trump since he will be able to ditch his ♣Q on the second trump).

Luckily, I see an option. I win the first trump in my hand and lead the ♥Q. When West's king covers, I play low from dummy. When West leads another trump, I win — East follows — and take the ♣AK. Both defenders follow, so I pitch my last club on the ♥A, ruff a club and reach dummy with a trump to discard two spades on the good clubs. I lose a spade at the end but we are +600. The full deal:

West	North	East
	♠ 7 4 ♥ A 5 3 ♦ A J 10 ♣ A K 7 6 5	
♠ A Q J 9 5 ♥ K J 6 4 ♦ 5 3 ♣ J 9	N W E S	♠ 10 8 2 ♥ 10 9 8 7 2 ♦ 9 7 ♣ Q 10 8
	♠ K 6 3 ♥ Q ♦ K Q 8 6 4 2 ♣ 4 3 2	

At the other table, North-South did well to get to 3NT after West's 1♠ opening. West stayed off a spade lead but he tried a low heart. Declarer was confident enough from the bidding that West had the ♥K that he played low from dummy, risking the contract. All was well; South's queen won. He cashed the next nine tricks for +630 and we lost an IMP.

Easley Blackwood called the loser-on-loser play declarer's 'faithful servant' because it has so many applications. It can be used to execute an endplay, to break the defenders' communication, to rectify the count for a squeeze or, as here, to establish a suit safely.

75

In a Regional Compact Knockout, my partner and I are an improvised partnership and have agreed on simple, old-fashioned bidding methods. On an early deal, both sides are vulnerable. As South, the dealer, I hold:

♠ A J 10 5
♡ 10 5 2
◇ A
♣ A Q J 8 5

I open 1♣, West overcalls 1♡ and my partner bids 2◇. East passes and I rebid 2♠. That's the cheapest bid I can make; hence, it is not a strength-showing reverse. My partner returns to 3♣.

I suppose that we might have no game. If partner's hearts are x-x-x or J-x-x, they could run the hearts against 3NT or beat 5♣ with three fast heart tricks. Partner might have a hand such as:

♠Q 4 ♡J 4 ◇K Q 7 6 5 ♣K 10 7 6

then, I would need a friendly diamond break or a winning spade finesse (not a favorite, perhaps, when West has overcalled) to make 5♣.

Still, when my hand is this strong, I think I would be putting partner under too much pressure if I bid only 4♣. I could bid 3♡, asking him to try 3NT with a heart stopper, but if his hand is:

♠Q 4 ♡K 4 ◇Q J 8 5 3 ♣K 10 9 3

we belong in 5♣, not 3NT; plus, with that hand, he might have bid 2NT instead of 3♣ anyway.

Hoping for good things, I jump to 5♣. All pass and West leads the ♡K.

Dlr: South Vul: Both	♠ K 3 2 ♡ Q 3 ♢ K 6 5 2 ♣ K 10 9 3
	♠ A J 10 5 ♡ 10 5 2 ♢ A ♣ A Q J 8 5

West	North	East	South
			1♣
1♡	2♢	pass	2♠
pass	3♣	pass	5♣
all pass			

Adherents of the game-forcing Two-over-One style would no doubt find our auction amusing — or appalling.

After West takes two top hearts, he shifts to the ♢10. I win and cash the ♣A and ♣10. East discards a heart. Seeking a count of the distribution that may help me locate the ♠Q, I discard a spade on the ♢K and ruff a diamond high. I draw the last trump with dummy's king and ruff the last diamond. Both defenders follow. When I ruff my last heart in dummy, East discards as expected.

Three tricks are left — I have the ♠K32 in dummy opposite my ♠AJ10 — but my guess in spades is a sure thing. I know West started with five hearts, four diamonds and three trumps, so only one spade. I can take the ♠K and lead to my jack, knowing the finesse will win unless West had fourteen cards. The full deal:

	♠ K 3 2 ♡ Q 3 ♢ K 6 5 2 ♣ K 10 9 3	
♠ 7 ♡ A K J 9 7 ♢ 10 9 8 4 ♣ 7 4 2	N W E S	♠ Q 9 8 6 4 ♡ 8 6 4 ♢ Q J 7 3 ♣ 6
	♠ A J 10 5 ♡ 10 5 2 ♢ A ♣ A Q J 8 5	

At the other table, South opened 1♣ again but my teammate in West was unwilling to overcall vulnerable. North responded 2NT, not forcing, showing about 11 points, balanced. I strongly dislike that treatment. If opener has a distributional hand, he won't want to sit 2NT; but he can't both force and sign off at the three-level.

South blithely raised to 3NT, passed out; but slapdash bidding was rewarded. East led a spade and North took eleven tricks for +660 and a 2-IMP loss for us. Justice is not always served.

76

At my partner's behest, I'm playing in a local Knockout Teams with handicaps. I suppose I'm too old-fashioned to appreciate the concept of handicapped events. Why players who have applied themselves to the game and achieved some success should be penalized by having to give IMPs to players less astute and diligent is beyond my understanding.*

My team has played well enough to overcome the handicap and is leading at the half. On the first deal after the break, only our side is vulnerable. As South, I hold:

♠ A 10 4 2
♡ A 8 2
◇ Q 9
♣ A 6 3 2

East deals and passes, I open 1♣ and North responds 1◇. Then East comes in with 1♠. At a different vulnerability, I might pursue a penalty. (I have talked my partner out of playing 'support doubles' but my hand isn't strong enough to double for penalty. I could, however, pass; if he reopened with a strength-showing double, I could pass it.) At this vulnerability, I will allow for reaching game, so I rebid 1NT.

My partner raises to 3NT and all pass. West ponders and leads the ♠5.

"All I have is a sound invitation," North shrugs as he tables the dummy, "but we're vulnerable and you did bid 1NT freely."

Dlr: East
Vul: N-S

♠ Q J 3
♡ J 5 3
◇ A K 10 8 7
♣ 5 4

♠ A 10 4 2
♡ A 8 2
◇ Q 9
♣ A 6 3 2

* When this deal appeared in the *Bridge Bulletin*, some readers objected to my comment about handicapped events. One reader cited the use of handicaps in golf. I have been a golfer for 60 years; I played first position on my college team and was close to scratch back then. All I can say is that I would take no pleasure, none at all, in 'winning' a match in which I was actually outscored by 10 shots.

West	North	East	South
		pass	1♣
pass	1♢	1♠	1NT
pass	3NT	all pass	

I can count eight tricks: three spades, three diamonds, the ♡A and the ♣A. I will be safe if I win four diamonds. Suppose I play the ♠Q from dummy. East will — or should — duck and I won't have an entry to the long diamond if the jack doesn't fall under the top honors. I do better to play the three from dummy.

East follows with the six and my ten wins. Now, if I continue with the ♢Q, ♢K and ♢A, I will make an overtrick if the jack falls but will otherwise have to concede the fourth diamond; then, a switch to clubs or hearts may set up too many tricks for the defense.

Fortunately, I see a solution. At the third trick, I let the ♢9 run. If East takes the jack, I can overtake my queen later. But the nine wins, so I can unblock the queen and lead a low spade to the queen, forcing an entry to dummy. East takes the ♠K and shifts to the ♣Q but I can win and cash out for +630. The full deal:

	North	
	♠ Q J 3 ♡ J 5 3 ♢ A K 10 8 7 ♣ 5 4	
West ♠ 5 ♡ Q 9 7 6 4 ♢ J 6 5 3 ♣ K 8 7	N W E S	**East** ♠ K 9 8 7 6 ♡ K 10 ♢ 4 2 ♣ Q J 10 9
	♠ A 10 4 2 ♡ A 8 2 ♢ Q 9 ♣ A 6 3 2	

At the other table, my teammate in East came in with that same filthy 1♠ overcall. What he hoped to achieve is a mystery. This time, South doubled for penalty, though how he expected to win seven tricks if North had nothing is another mystery. North was happy to pass. After South led the ♢Q, the defense won nine tricks for +500 but we gained 4 IMPs.

At my table, North attached some significance to my 'free bid' of 1NT — rightly, I think. He expected me to have more than a minimum or average hand. Many experts have abandoned the free-bid concept and rebid good long suits despite a high-card minimum. In this situation, a free 1NT bid should suggest soundness. A minimum balanced hand can pass.

North's raise to 3NT was aggressive but, since we were vulnerable, with more to gain by making a game, he chose an aggressive game try: Bid game and try to make it.

77

In a Sectional Swiss Teams, my team has won its first two matches but by narrow margins. In our third match, the opening deal appears to be flat and then, with neither side vulnerable, I pick up:

♠ K Q 10 6 4 2
♡ 7 2
♢ A Q 2
♣ Q 4

West, the dealer, opens 1NT, showing a good 15 to 18 points in their style, and East responds 2♢, a transfer to hearts. I suppose I could pass. If West accepts the transfer with 2♡, and two passes follow, I could back in with 2♠. But there exists an outside chance that we have a game and we'll never get there unless I bid directly. So, I climb in with 2♠. I hope my partner will infer that I have a decent hand and am not 'pre-balancing' with long spades and little else.

Somewhat to my surprise, everyone passes and West leads the ♣K.

Dlr: West
Vul: None

♠ A 9
♡ J 6 3
♢ 7 6 5 3
♣ 8 5 3 2

♠ K Q 10 6 4 2
♡ 7 2
♢ A Q 2
♣ Q 4

West	North	East	South
1NT	pass	2♢	2♠
all pass			

East follows with the six and West continues with the ♣A and a third club: five, jack, ruff by me. I shouldn't have harbored any thoughts of making a game; I have my hands full taking eight tricks. I've lost two clubs and have two hearts to lose, plus at least one diamond; what's more, the trumps are not even certain to break.

Let me make some assumptions. East must have at least one heart honor. If West had had the ♡AKQ, he would have led a high heart; plus, I suspect he would have competed to 3♡. In that case, West is marked with the ◇K. I suppose he could have:

♠J 8 7 ♡A Q 8 ◇J 9 8 ♣A K 10 7

but that doesn't look like a 'good' 15 to me; and such a specific holding is against the odds, anyway.

It seems that if I'm to lose only one diamond, I need to find West with ◇Kx. But I know his clubs were AK107 and I'm almost sure he had three hearts. If East had had a six-card heart suit and a few values, he could have competed to the three-level. So, to have a chance, I give West 4-3-2-4 shape.

On the fourth trick, I lead a trump to dummy's nine. West follows low so next I take the ace and East discards a heart. I lead back to my ◇A, draw trumps with the ♠KQ and lead a low diamond. When West's king appears, my eight tricks are safely in the bag and we are +110. The full deal:

	North	
	♠ A 9 ♡ J 6 3 ◇ 7 6 5 3 ♣ 8 5 3 2	
West ♠ J 8 7 3 ♡ K Q 8 ◇ K 10 ♣ A K 10 7	N W E S	**East** ♠ 5 ♡ A 10 9 5 4 ◇ J 9 8 4 ♣ J 9 6
	♠ K Q 10 6 4 2 ♡ 7 2 ◇ A Q 2 ♣ Q 4	

This was a deal for one of Terence Reese's 'second-degree assumptions'. I assumed that one suit lay favorably and followed the consequences of my assumption.

At the other table, the auction started the same way but the East on my team refused to sell out to 2♠. He competed with 3♦, West returned to 3♥ and everyone passed. (Most pairs treat a new-suit bid after a transfer as forcing. I prefer a new suit to be invitational, to facilitate accurate game bidding. In a competitive auction, I would think East's 3♦ certainly should not be forcing.)

Against 3♥, North led the ♠A and a second spade. Declarer ruffed in dummy, picked up the clubs, drew trumps and led toward the ♦K to make ten tricks. (He could have made eleven.)

My teammates weren't happy to be +170. East thought West should have competed with 3♥ over 2♠. Failing that, East maintained, West should have bid 4♥ over 3♦. The fact that we gained 7 IMPs anyway wasn't quite enough to salve their feelings.

78

In a Sectional Swiss Teams, our opponents are a Flight A pair. As South, the dealer, with both sides vulnerable, I hold:

♠ A K Q J 6
♡ A K
◇ 7 4
♣ J 8 4 2

I open 1♠ and my partner raises to 2♠. This hand isn't worth its point count. My ♠J is a wasted point since I can probably draw trumps without it. My hand would be better if I could trade in my two jacks for the ♣Q. Still, I can't take a conservative view when we're vulnerable at IMPs; I jump to 4♠ and everyone passes.

West leads a trump and, though dummy produces two aces, it's not to my liking.

Dlr: South
Vul: Both

North:
♠ 10 9 4
♡ 9 4 3
◇ A 6 5 2
♣ A 5 3

South:
♠ A K Q J 6
♡ A K
◇ 7 4
♣ J 8 4 2

West	North	East	South
			1♠
pass	2♠	pass	4♠
all pass			

I have gotten us into the wrong contract and this trump lead is trouble-some. On a heart lead, I would have had time to ruff my fourth club in dummy. As it is, suppose I cash the ♣A and concede a club. The defense will win and lead a second trump. Then, if I concede another club, the defense can lead a third trump, leaving dummy with none, and if the clubs lie badly, my fourth club will be a loser.

Can I do anything about that? Dummy's trump spots are attractive, so maybe I need not rely on a club ruff. I win the first trump in my hand with the ace, cash the ♡AK and duck a diamond. West wins and leads a second trump and I let dummy's ten win. East discards a heart.

Next, I ruff a heart, cross to the ◊A, ruff a diamond, return to the ♣A and ruff the last diamond. I have won nine tricks — two high trumps, two high hearts, the ◊A, the ♣A and three ruffs in my hand — and dummy still has the ♠9 to fulfill the contract. If I had pursued a club ruff in dummy, I would have failed since the full deal is:

West	North / South	East
	♠ 10 9 4 ♡ 9 4 3 ◊ A 6 5 2 ♣ A 5 3	
♠ 8 5 3 2 ♡ J 8 6 ◊ Q 10 ♣ K Q 9 7	N W E S	♠ 7 ♡ Q 10 7 5 2 ◊ K J 9 8 3 ♣ 10 6
	♠ A K Q J 6 ♡ A K ◊ 7 4 ♣ J 8 4 2	

At the other table, South's judgment was better than mine. Over North's raise to 2♠, South probed with a bid of 3♣. When North continued with 3◊, South tried 3NT. North was happy to pass that and there were nine top tricks. Still, our +620 was good enough for a 1-IMP gain and an IMP is an IMP.

79

In a Regional Swiss Teams with eight matches, my team has suffered one loss in the first session and can't afford any more. In the first match after the break, both sides are vulnerable and, as North, the dealer, I hold:

♠ Q 10
♡ A K 3 2
◇ Q J 10 9 7 3
♣ A

I open 1◇, my partner responds 1♠ and I bid 2♡. In the style I prefer, a reverse suggests a bit more high-card strength than I hold but I'm willing to stretch here. The good six-card suit is compensation. My alternative, a jump to 3◇, might lose the heart suit and might make it harder for us to get to 3NT if that contract is best. If my partner has a weak hand, we have methods that will let us get out below game.

Partner next bids 3NT. That bid shows no interest in any other contract; if he wanted to investigate slam or game in a major suit or in diamonds, he would do something different. So I pass trustingly.

West leads the ♣J and I put down my dummy and let my thoughts drift away from the table. On the last day of a tournament, stamina is a factor and following partner's dummy play will only drain my reservoir of mental energy. I'll let you see the problem he faced:

Dlr: North
Vul: Both

North:
♠ Q 10
♡ A K 3 2
◇ Q J 10 9 7 3
♣ A

South:
♠ K J 9 8 4
♡ 9 4
◇ 8 5 4
♣ K Q 7

West	North	East	South
	1◇	pass	1♠
pass	2♡	pass	3NT
all pass			

After South takes the ♣A, how should he continue?

South correctly started on the diamonds. If the defense won and continued clubs, South would be safe by forcing out the other high diamond. He would have four diamonds, two clubs and two hearts and would have time to set up his ninth trick in spades. But when West won the first diamond with the king, he shifted to the ♡J. My partner realized that if he won that and led a second diamond, he might be in trouble. The defense would win and force out dummy's second high heart. Declarer would have only eight tricks and when the defense took the ♠A, they might cash two hearts.

So, after South took the ♡A, he led dummy's ♠Q. The full deal:

	♠ Q 10 ♡ A K 3 2 ◇ Q J 10 9 7 3 ♣ A	
♠ 7 5 2 ♡ J 10 6 ◇ K 2 ♣ J 10 9 6 3	N W E S	♠ A 6 3 ♡ Q 8 7 5 ◇ A 6 ♣ 8 5 4 2
	♠ K J 9 8 4 ♡ 9 4 ◇ 8 5 4 ♣ K Q 7	

East had to play low. If he took the ace, declarer would have four spades, two hearts and three clubs. So, declarer overtook with the ♠K, cashed the ♣K and led another diamond. He was sure to make four diamonds, two hearts, two clubs and a spade for +600.

My partner's careful play gained nothing. In fact, we lost an IMP on the board. The auction at the other table was 1◇-1♠, 3◇-3♠, 4♠. With spades breaking well and no diamond ruff available to the defenders, declarer lost just two diamonds and spade for +620.

80

This is a deal that caused a protracted discussion in a Sectional Knockout Teams. South was the dealer with both sides vulnerable. At my table, I was West, a bystander. The North-South cards were:

♠ 7 6 5
♡ A Q 10 9
◇ Q 10 8
♣ J 10 3

♠ J 9
♡ J
◇ A K J 9 7 4
♣ A K 9 4

West	North	East	South
			1◇
pass	1♡	pass	3◇
pass	4◇	pass	pass(!)
all pass			

Our opponents bid timidly — some would say wrongly. I could make a case for North's 4◇ raise to be a chance-giving action; but most experts would have treated it as forcing. We led spades and declarer ruffed the third spade, drew trumps and took the club finesse. It lost and he claimed for +130, an uncertain result both for our opponents and us.

At the other table, my teammates climbed up to game.

West	North	East	South
			1◇
pass	1♡	pass	2♣
pass	2◇	pass	3◇
pass	4◇	pass	5◇
all pass			

South's 2♣ rebid was more flexible than the jump to 3◇ made at my table. His third-round 3◇ suggested a shapely hand — probably with six diamonds and four clubs — as well as game interest.

West led the ♠2 and East took the king and ace and led a third spade, ruffed. Declarer then drew trumps with the ◇A and ◇J. How should he continue?

South went for a combination shot. He cashed the ♣AK. Both defenders played low, so South led his ♡J to the ace and returned the queen for a ruffing finesse. When East didn't play the king, South discarded a club. Alas for him, West took the ♡K — and cashed the ♣Q. We lost 8 IMPs. The full deal was:

	♠ 7 6 5 ♡ A Q 10 9 ◇ Q 10 8 ♣ J 10 3	
♠ Q 10 4 2 ♡ K 8 7 6 ◇ 5 3 ♣ Q 5 2	N W E S	♠ A K 8 3 ♡ 5 4 3 2 ◇ 6 2 ♣ 8 7 6
	♠ J 9 ♡ J ◇ A K J 9 7 4 ♣ A K 9 4	

Then came the discussion. North wasn't so annoyed that South had gone down, though he noted the contract could have been made with a heart-club squeeze against West. (After the defense took two spades, they could have broken up the squeeze with a heart shift.) What rankled North was that South had gone down two. North contended that cashing the top clubs first was unjustified because it might (and did) result in a second undertrick.

If our declarer had either finessed in clubs or taken the ruffing heart finesse, he would have been only -100 and we would have lost 6 IMPs instead of 8. If, at my table, the contract had been 5◇ and declarer had played for only one chance, we would have lost 3 IMPs. Neither of those scenarios seems too significant. My teammate's play stood to gain 10 IMPs.

I'm not much of a mathematician. A defender will hold Qx in clubs about 16% of the time but, as far as I can tell, if the deal were played 100 times, trying both chances would show a gain of several thousand points — a bundle of IMPs.

I will say this. Dummy play involves more than cold numbers. The adverse psychological effect on a player and a partnership is significant when declarer goes down in a makeable game — whether he goes down one or two. For the sake of partnership morale, I believe that declarer should make the best play, within reason, to make the contract.

About the author

Frank Stewart (b. 1946) is one of the world's most prolific bridge journalists, known as an advocate of a sound and disciplined approach to bidding. He won many tournament events before devoting himself to writing. Stewart served as co-editor of the ACBL's *Bridge Bulletin* from 1984 to 1989 and continues to contribute through an instructional column he started in 1981. He edited the ACBL's World Championship books from 1983 to 1987 and was a principal contributor from 1986 to 1989. He was also a principal contributor to the Fifth Edition of *The Official Encyclopedia of Bridge*.

In 1986, Stewart began a collaboration with Alfred Sheinwold to produce the famous syndicated newspaper column 'Sheinwold on Bridge'. After Sheinwold's death in 1997, the column continued under Stewart's byline as 'Sheinwold's Bridge' and in 2000, became the 'Daily Bridge Club'. It appears in newspapers worldwide and on major internet sites.

Stewart has published hundreds of magazine and online articles, including technical pieces, tournament reports, fiction and humor. He has written twenty-four other books, among them *Becoming an Expert*, *Who Has the Queen?*, *What's Your Call?* and *Frank Stewart's Bridge Club*. He is a senior analyst for ACBL-wide Charity and International Fund events, having served since 1980.

Stewart has been honored by the Birmingham AL Duplicate Bridge Club, of which he is a supporter and a member. The club houses the Frank Stewart Library, which was facilitated by a donation of books and materials from him. In 2005, the club established a trophy in his name for a Sectional Swiss Teams.

In 2014, Frank Stewart received the International Bridge Press Association's Truscott Award for achievements that Alan Truscott, the former bridge editor of the New York Times, would appreciate.

Stewart is a graduate of the University of Alabama, where he studied Voice and Musicology. He is a low-handicap golfer and a past chairman of the Fayette Christian Center of Concern, a food bank. He and his wife, Charlotte, a pediatric speech pathologist, live in Fayette, Alabama. They have a twenty-two-year-old daughter.